First edition published 2017
by Stories of Oz Publishing
PO Box K57
Haymarket NSW 1240

ABN: 0920230558
facebook.com/storiesofoz
ozbookstore.com

ISBN: 978-0-6480627-6-9

Cover image photography: Steve Flockton
Typeset in Segoe UI and Century Gothic

FISHING FROM SYDNEY TO BRISBANE

STEVE FLOCKTON

CONTENTS

BASS ON LURES

The Australian bass is a hard fighting little sportfish said to grow to 65cm, available in virtually all of the eastern flowing freshwater creeks, streams and rivers from Northern Victoria to Southern Queensland. Between Sydney and Brisbane is considered by many as the 'heartland' of bass fishing.

Bass are natives and a lot of dams have been stocked by hatchery-bred fish. This is an on-going process because bass need to go to saltwater to breed. Anglers working rivers and creeks catch fish from wild stocks and it's this side of bass fishing I'm concentrating on.

Once you get into bass fishing it doesn't take long to realise that they live in quite a restricted environment. If fishing pressure was somehow worked out per cubic metre of water available to the species, the results would surprise many anglers. Good looking bass water gets worked on a regular basis and if everyone kept the fish they caught, wild stocks would soon become scarce.

Thankfully, the majority of anglers, both local and visitors, do so on a catch and release basis. Strictly speaking there is a bag and size limit on bass but keeping them for the table is a sure-fire way of enduring the wrath of fellow anglers. I'm proud of the way fisherman protect their bass. Anglers are increasingly being told what they can and cannot do by new and stricter laws, yet with bass the majority have voluntarily taken a much more conservative approach, by releasing every fish caught, often using barbless hooks to minimise damage to the fish.

Bass fishing takes you into excellent country.

All big bass are females and these fish produce our future stocks. Human nature being what it is means that when a big fish is landed, the natural reaction is to keep it to show friends and family as proof of the capture. The way around this is to take a few photos. These days everyone's phone has a camera. They are simple to use and you get a really good photo when the fish is alive with the beautiful background of the environment you caught it in. Camera conservation gives a permanent record and years later it's nice to know that fish is most likely still swimming.

The most common description of a bass's size is by length. Any bass longer than a fish measuring stick (i.e. 38 cm) is a good one. 50cm is the bench mark that many anglers aspire to, yet not too many get there.

A nice bass coming to the boat.

While they can be caught from the shore, most anglers use a canoe, kayak or small boat. This gives access to water that receives less pressure and hopefully holds more fish. Bass are not too keen on screaming outboards and better results come from the use of an electric motor or paddles. There are specialised bass boats on the market that let you fish in comfort and if you can afford one that's great. Otherwise any small craft that doesn't leak too much and has a shallow draught will do the job.

Light whippy rods between 1.5 to 2 metres in length, matched to either a small overhead or eggbeater reel are the standard gear. The outfit should be able to cast reasonably light lures and if you have any doubt about a rod then go for a lighter model. Pistol grip rods are a popular choice with over-head reels due to their single-handed casting design, although a rod with a short butt will do the same job. Years ago, overheads were standard for the majority of bass fisherman, but now little eggbeaters are more popular.

Bass can be caught on light line, but today's trend is moving towards heavier line for a quicker capture so the fish is healthier upon release. Heavier line is also handy for pulling lures out of trees. The standard practice is to get your lure as close to structure as possible because that is where the fish are, so it makes little sense to use excessively light line when they can, and often do, wrap around a log or sticks less than a metre from where they originally took the lure. 2 kilo line should be considered as light, 4-6 kilo average and 8 kilo as heavy.

In order to breed, bass move downstream into brackish and saltwater in the

A lovely early morning bass.

autumn months and return during spring. In NSW while it is not law, most bass fish-erman leave them alone during this period, as they believe that when females with roe (eggs) are stressed, they absorb the eggs back into their body and that year's breeding is wasted. I do not know if this is fact or folklore. My personal opin-ion is that with good fish handling practices the chance of over stressing them is low, yet I also give them a rest until they are back in the freshwater reaches. For both states September is the start of the bass season.

PRIME TIME

Bass can occasionally be caught at any time of day, but by far the most pro-ductive times are early morning, late afternoon and into the night. Morning outings can start while it's still dark and generally go for a few hours after sunrise. The amount of time the fish will stay on the bite depends on weather conditions. If the sun hits the water early then chances are the bass in that location will also go off the bite early. An exception to this 'rule' is with lily pads because bass love to hide in their shade and ambush bugs that fall off them. The best way to find bass when the sun is up high is to target water that has shade on it. Foggy or heavy overcast conditions tend to help the fish stay interested for longer.

Reviving the fish before release. Note the barb at the end of the gill plate, it is sharp.

If it were possible to order ideal weather conditions, I'd go for no wind and a heavy fog during the morning. Afternoons fire up earlier when there is good cloud cover, while starlit nights with a good moon are ideal. I prefer no wind because it is easier, but the bass don't mind it. Some of my best sessions have been in windy conditions where you can only manage one or two casts before getting blown into the bank. The bass were on that side of the creek waiting for cicadas and bugs to get blown across the top towards them, so they were really aggressive on surface lures as well. They are not nearly as timid when there is a ruffle on the water and I think it also makes it harder for them to see you.

FISHING STYLE

Bass can be caught on bait, lures and flies. Lure casting is by far the most popular but whatever style you use the basics are very similar. All things have to be put close to where the fish are to get results. Bass are very structure orientated, preferring to hang in tight to underwater logs, deep bank walls, under lily pads plus around snags, fallen trees and rock bars. The base of a large tree on the edge of the bank is also a good spot to target, as there is often deep water beside them. Sometimes the current undermines these large trees resulting in a huge labyrinth of tree roots under the water line. This makes an excellent ambush site for the predatory bass and if you can get your first cast right in close, the chances of a strike are high.

Bass have a pecking order when it comes to who occupies the best ambush site or snag. Bigger fish bully smaller ones away and it is often found that the biggest fish are at the snags that provide the best shelter and food. This knowledge can be put to good use when you get a creek wired because sites where solid fish were previously caught have an excellent chance of producing again. Some snags are obvious fish holders, generally where a large tree has fallen into a

Bass don't have teeth so metal lip grips are not really needed. (Photo by C. Garrick)

deep section and there are no other visible snags on that stretch of waterway.

These places deserve a good work over and don't be scared to try different style lures to work different depths. With big snags such as a large fallen tree there are plenty of places to pop a lure. I prefer to start at the tree's base as there is often a good hole under there and if it's a good cast with the lure right in tight, I'll use the non-retrieve. (More later) If that doesn't work a lure wiggled down deeper along the tree trunk is the next best thing and if boat positioning allows, it can be done on the same cast.

To work the head of a tree (the branchy part) I prefer using a surface crawler because they catch fewer snags and tend to bring the fish to the top where you have a much better chance of getting them out of the timber. Another alternative is to use a floating diving lure and work it very slowly through the sunken branches. If you run into trouble, and you will, stop winding and lower the rod tip. Most times this will release the lure and let it float back to the surface.

Fishing from the bank is harder, but can be rewarding.

On most parts of the coast there is no shortage of snags and you will often find yourself fishing areas that have heaps of tiger country. Finding bass in water that is over populated with good-looking spots can be difficult, especially if you don't know the creek or river. Mostly it's a case of working the water, moving from place to place until you find the fish. Often they are scattered over a wide region while other times a single stretch of water will be the most productive.

Sometimes a place will only produce well during certain times of the year. I have fond memories of an overhanging

Prior to capture this fish was aggressively feeding off the surface.

wattle tree that was guaranteed a crashing strike on the first well placed lure. When the tree was in flower it was dynamite but when the flowers were gone so were the bass. The fish had been attracted to the spot by the insects drawn by the flowers. The fish were tuned into expecting food like bees, beetles and bugs to fall out of the tree and onto the water. So when a lure

13

splashed down they crashed it with lightning speed. Even though the water was completely fresh, I pulled a few good bream from under the same tree and they hit the lure the same way as the bass, the instant it touched down.

THE NON-RETRIEVE

The non-retrieve style of lure tossing is as the name implies you cast the lure to where you want it and instead of instantly cranking it back, you leave it there for a while. Once you have left it still for ten or twenty seconds give the lure signs of life by gently twitching the rod tip. The lure should put out a ring of disturbance in the water and the trebles will shake like little legs. This is often when the lure is crashed because the fish think it is something alive and therefore edible. The actual amount of time you leave a lure in a certain spot depends on the current and also how 'fishy' you think that spot is. Lures are best retrieved once they have floated out of the strike zone.

Kayaks are great platforms for sneaking up on fish.

This style works best during summer when the fish are expecting beetles, cicadas and grasshoppers etc to fall into the water. To be successful the lure has to be where you would expect these insects to fall. Places such as overhanging branches, undercut banks and large trees growing close to the bank, especially if they have been eroded by the current.

Unless you are super accurate this is not a style to use on every cast. To get the best out of non-retrieve fishing, the lure must land in a top spot where there is a big chance of a fish. There is nothing to be gained by allowing a lure to float aimlessly three metres away from your target. It still may get hit, but the chances are slim.

An important thing to remember when using surface crawlers or a floating diver that has just splashed down and been clobbered, is to not strike hard with the rod. You can pick up loose line but let the bass load the rod. It can be hard, but try to resist striking them when a lure's on the surface because if you don't hook-up you could rocket the lure back into your face. It's safer to crank the reel and 'wind' them onto the hooks rather than striking.

It doesn't get much better than quality fish,
beautiful country and yaking with your mates.

SURFACE LURES

Surface lures are designed to chug and paddle their way across the top of the water and bass definitely like them. They can be very effective during the day and just on dark and into the night is when they perform their best.

Lures such as crazy crawlers, jitterbugs, poppers and splashers are all designed to work the surface. At night I prefer the style that has a cupped and chromed splash plate on the front of the lure. These pick up the light and flash it into the water which seems to help attract the bass's attention. They will even flick around light off a big moon. I don't worry too much about colours but I have to admit a liking for black because as strange as it sounds, black shows a stronger silhouette at night.

To get the most out of surface crawlers it is important to get their action right. If you wind too fast they will skitter across the surface, which is pretty useless on bass as they like a slower retrieve. The right speed is when the lure makes a plop plop, plop, plop, sound caused by the lure rolling from side to side as the splash plate digs into the water.

A yellow cicada surface lure brought this fish undone.

The water is not really being splashed by the lure; it's more of a disturbance than a splash. You can hear when a surface lure is working correctly and when the surroundings are quiet these lures make a fair noise.

Some anglers prefer to make their own surface lures. Often they are works of art adorned with eyes, feelers, feathery tails and a sharp hook. They work surprisingly well, even the ones that don't look a picture will catch bass if

When cicadas are screaming it's a great time for surface lures.

they are put in the right spot. I once met a bloke who made his own lures out of thongs that were real classics. Instead of having the hooks down in the water, he had weighted the body so a single barbless hook always stuck out in the air on top of the lure. He reckoned the hook-up rate wasn't real flash but that didn't matter, he was chasing multiple strikes. For him the thrill was in his lure technique, fooling the fish into trying to eat his lure while still being in with a chance to catch it.

A cicada surface lure fooled this nice bass.

I've had a lot of success working a surface lure along the edges of lily pads and also dropping a lure in clear patches among the lilies and leaving it there for a minute or two. Of all the styles available to catch bass, surface lures are the most addictive. The shock value of a strike is doubled when your lure is crashed with a huge surface eruption.

DIVING LURES

Bass take a wide range of diving lures, with floating minnows being the most popular amongst anglers. Generally speaking these lures are approximately 5cm to 7cm long (2 or 3 inches) without the bib. There is a huge list of brand-name lures that catch bass in a wide range of colours. It's more important where you put the lure and how it is worked, rather than its name. Having said that, on many parts of the coast there is a strong cottage industry making bass lures designed specifically for local conditions. If for example you were on holidays in a new area, local lure makers have probably tested their lures in the same water you intend to fish. Getting onto Facebook on some of the bass sites is an easy way to find local lure makers.

17

While the average sized lure used is 5 to 7cm, bass will hit lures twice this size. A lot of bass anglers will dispute that statement, mainly because they

haven't tried it. Bass are a terribly aggressive fish when they get their hackles up and they'll have a go at things that are really quite big when compared to themselves. When you think about it, a hungry and/or angry 40cm bass is not going to be scared by a 15cm lure and it could be just the thing to induce a strike. Big lures are used specifically for targeting big fish although you can still catch big bass on normal sized lures. I'm not advocating a radi-

A diving lure is an excellent choice on early season bass.

cal change in lure sizes but given the choice between a 5cm and an 8cm lure, I'd take the 8.

Bass will hit a diving lure any time between splash-down and when it reaches the rod tip. Most strikes occur fairly early in the retrieve as the lure is working better water. Yet sometimes they come well away from cover and shadow the lure right up to the boat.

Retrieval speed is reasonably slow. The idea is to get the lure's action working at an easy pace rather than a faster one. Today's reels are often high geared and it is easy to gain line too fast when you get into a mechanical cast and retrieve routine. I regularly catch myself winding too fast and often have to make a conscious effort to slow down.

NIGHT FISHING

Tossing lures at night is a great way of dodging the heat of summer and it can also be extremely productive. Nights are generally less noisy, and areas that experience reasonable daytime boating traffic and give the impression of being fished out often come alive after dark.

During the day casting accurately right in close to cover is the way to go, but at night it is simply impossible to pop a lure within centimetres of a snag or the bank when you can hardly even see it in the first place. Thankfully, while bass are a very cover orientated fish, they do tend to venture into clean water at night. This is not to say they all go cruising snag free water, but they do move around a bit once the light level drops.

Trying to land lures really close to structures at night can make the outing an incredibly frustrating experience. Getting lures out of trees during the day is bad enough and at night it's twice as bad, especially if you are in a canoe or kayak and the lure is high. To keep the stress levels down I purposely drop the lure short of the target and still manage to catch enough fish to stay happy. It's also easier to start a night outing before it gets dark as it helps to fine tune your casting arm and allows you to get the feel of the area and distances to the bank.

Late afternoon is prime bass time.

When night fishing with an overhead it's handy to throw the occasional long cast out into open water. This removes any loose loops of line from the spool, which could cause a backlash on a future cast. You don't pick up many fish on these long shots but when you do it's good fun, especially if they are big. Another trick with overheads at night is to crank up the magnetic spool control to help stop overruns. This is especially important if you have been fuzzing the reel on earlier casts because at night, making sense out of a reel that resembles a bird's nest can be frustrating and sometimes impossible. If constant fuzzing or back-lashing of the reel is occurring then chances are the end plate adjustment needs tightening as well.

This fish was still feeding on a bright sunny day.

For exhilarating adrenalin-pumping action, surface lures at night are hard to beat. Because the lure is on top and the bass attacks from underneath, the strike is spectacular. If there is any moon you will see the strike, if not you will certainly hear it. Sometimes bass wait until the very last second before hammering the lure and these hits are guaranteed to get the blood pumping. On a number of occasions we have been wet by bass exploding a lure at the side of the canoe and it never fails to scare the hell out of us. Often these close encounters don't hook-up, but at the time it doesn't seem to matter.

Some nights bass are not in a feeding mood yet they can still be quite aggressive and great fun on lures. Instead of trying for a feed they slap at the lure to get it out of their territory. Under these circumstances any bass landed is hooked on the outside of the mouth, although generally speaking when bass are in a slapping mood very few fish are caught. When they really get into it scoring 8 or 10 splashing strikes on one cast is not out of the question. Obviously this doesn't happen every outing but when it does it burns into your memory.

We have had a few times where the bass were pumped up and incredibly aggro. Mostly it has started about an hour after dark with absolutely no warning and lasted for 2 or 3 hours before suddenly going off. Unfortunately we didn't know what the barometer was doing at the time and apart from that I have no idea why they ran amok in the first place, then instantly stopped.

A quality early morning fish.

BAROMETRIC PRESSURE

I have to confess to doing well over twenty-five years of bass fishing before bothering about barometric pressure and the way it affects them. I still haven't come to any solid conclusions worthy of putting into print so here is the general consensus of other writers.

Any barometric pressure over 1010 hPa is worth a try. Preference should be given to a rising barometer, especially if it is pushing over 1020, as this is when they really get active. Approaching storms have a habit of getting bass in a striking mood and while I don't know what it does to a barometer, I suspect the movement is sharp and that is what gets the bass going. A rising barometer after long periods of low pressure is also a good time to fish. One thing's for sure, no matter what the barometer is doing; if you don't go fishing you will never catch them.

HUNTING STYLE

To successfully chase bass a hunting style should be adopted. You have to find these fish before you can catch them, and even then it pays to keep moving because they quickly become lure shy when one or two of their mates have been pulled off the one snag.

You don't have to be ultra quiet but it sure helps in the confined space of a creek. Sneaking up on a snag and landing the first cast right in close is the best way I know of for getting results. Some days it doesn't have to be the first cast for success, but a lot of days it does. I think it gets back to the fact that bass see a fair amount of lures and often it takes something a bit special to con them.

Unless they are landlocked, most bass are not resident fish. They move down to saltwater to breed and once they are on their way back they keep slowly moving upstream until something stops them such as a rock bar or a waterfall, or even the urge to move back to saltwater for breeding. During the season if a part of the waterway that has been producing for weeks goes quiet, chances are they have moved upstream.

CONCLUSION

Bass are not hard to catch. You can score a strike on the first cast or it may take hours. It all depends on where you put the lure and how the fish are feeling. The deal with chasing bass is, it's often more of a nature walkabout than a brag about numbers of fish caught.

Don't be too downhearted when a local angler tells you that 'his' waterway has very few bass and you would be far better off fishing another river for good results. This is a regular occurrence that has been going on for years. A good example is when anglers on the Macleay River regularly tell visitors that the Clarence River is heaps more productive, yet you get to the Clarence and locals will tell you the Macleay is far better! This yarn spinning is really a case of protecting their own water from outsiders who may pillage their bass.

Canoeing, kayaking or small boating the numerous creeks and rivers will certainly put you into beautiful country ranging from open farmland to thick rainforest. Many of the waterways have bush frontage and it's not hard to get away from civilisation.

The water is clean (unless there is heavy rain) and generally there is an abundance of snags and good-looking water. It's still possible to catch bass over 50cm but it doesn't happen too often. When it does, it is hoped the lucky angler realises the privilege of encountering such a big female and releases her unharmed for future fish stocks and other lucky anglers. If you have never released one then give it a go. I guarantee you'll get a warm glow from the experience.

ARTIFICIALS IN THE ESTUARY

There are a huge number of estuary systems on this part of the coast. You don't have to travel far to find one and they all produce fish. Bream and flathead are the most common species caught and once you hit the warmer waters there are plenty of other lure crunchers available. For ease of writing I have combined lures and soft plastics together and almost always call them lures. While they are different to look at, they are both artificial and still have to be put in the same places to catch fish.

To really go deep into the subject would make the other chapters look tiny so I won't do it. Besides, once you get an idea of what you are doing it's easy. It's also a remarkably enjoyable way of spending a few hours on the water. If you have never tried lure fishing in an estuary then you may have deep seated or preconceived idea's about it's worth. This is not a hairy fairy idea dreamed up by the trendies. You can catch fish on them and for daytime, more often than not they are more productive than baits, especially in hard-fished waters. Plenty of fishing competitions in estuaries are won by lure fisherman. These anglers are often good all-rounders who work hard at what they are doing. They're after results and if these things didn't produce they wouldn't use them.

This little jew took a lure intended for something much bigger

In southern estuaries when using minnow lures I find areas away from the river mouth are the most productive for bream and flathead. This is possibly due to water depth although I think the different environment has a bit to do with it. Even so, I've caught a number of bream on bait jigs off river breakwalls and they also like small plastics. Larger plastics worked down the edge of a breakwall can be deadly on flathead and jew. So while plastics work well around the river mouth, small minnows don't.

Better areas to try with minnows are around sand and mud flats, oyster leases, mangroves, creek mouths and further up river close to the bank and other structures. Often the current is not nearly as savage and when an extremely low tide is in progress there is far less water for fish to hide in.

BREAM

For many anglers the idea of catching bream on lures is something of a novelty. Yet there is nothing new about it as anglers have been doing it for at least the last 30 years and probably longer.

Early mornings are great on the water, especially when bream are biting.

I suspect bass fisherman were the first to discover that bream are susceptible to lures. Bream often move up into freshwater and just like bass they feed on what is available. Actually bream and bass have a lot in common as far as lure fishing is concerned. They both like structures, both are aggressive and they take the same lures, although bream do prefer a slightly smaller lure than bass. If you haven't read the bass chapter I suggest you do because a lot of the information is also relevant to bream.

The biggest hurdle for bait fisherman new to the game is to realise that bream are a predatory fish capable of hunting down their food. Anglers live baiting with herring know only too well about the attacking ability of bream. Sometimes using live herring is a waste of time because bream kill the herring minutes after they hit the water.

Black lures often get the job done.

When bait fishing for bream in quiet estuarine waters they can be an incredibly finicky fish, suspiciously probing and bumping at a bait before deciding whether to actually eat it. This gives a false impression of bream being timid, because they have a darker side and lures often bring their predator instincts to the boil.

Bream give an honest fight and have enough power to turn a canoe or kayak in the direction of the cover they are running towards. Their first run is the strongest and after that they ease off into shorter bursts. If they don't run you into a snag on the first attempt there is a very good chance the fish will be landed. After their initial scare, big bream tend to cruise and use their bulky body to good effect by staying side-on to the angler.

I tend to drift from one style to another depending on the season and how I'm feeling. It's not always about catching numbers either.

A cicada surface lure fooled this bream.

The last few years amongst other styles, I've targeted bream with surface lures using a kayak to quietly hunt them down. It is a really challenging sport that I enjoy, and I'm getting better at it!

They never fail to amaze me with the different ways they take the lure. Sometimes you get a few in a row where they are quietly slurping the lure off the top with hardly a ripple showing. Then the next strike is a massively aggressive hit with plenty of white water. It makes you think it has to be a mangrove jack, but so far they have all been bream.

FLATHEAD

Flathead are well known lure crunchers and while they slow up during colder months, they hit them all year. Warmer months are the most productive and on the first few hot days in August or early September they often bite with a vengeance. June and July are possibly the worst months, although the odd one still gets caught.

If you have only experienced them in an offshore situation then you are in for a shock. Offshore flathead are slugs to catch with very little fight in them.

Yet in estuaries they are a totally different proposition. If the fish has any size about it you get a good fight and in the shallows they occasionally jump clear out of the water.

The most common-sized flathead ranges from under-sized to about 45 cm,

A chunky flathead caught from the bank

although much larger specimens are not too uncommon. Dusky flathead have been recorded to approximately 15 kilo and 1.3 metres in length. Any flathead over one and a half kilo can safely be assumed as female because males are not that big.

Flathead are often referred to as lizards, or when they are really big, crocodiles. A fair number of anglers see them in the crocodile range but not too many actually land the fish. This is because of the big flathead's fighting style. Often they come to the boat with deceptive ease, give you a blast of adrenalin with a glimpse of their shovel-sized head, and then blast off at warp speed with a powerful run. They don't run far but they take off incredibly quick and if the drag is a touch too tight or a bit lumpy, they'll bust the line quick smart. Compounding the problem is the fact that big flathead often inhale little lures and plastics deep into their mouth allowing the line to rub against their teeth. This frays the line, which can dramatically reduce its breaking strain.

Be extremely careful when you can feel that whatever you have hooked has good weight but comes in a bit too easy. This is their main tactic for escape and many times they cruise rather than fight, conserving energy for an explosive run close to the boat. After they've seen the boat and you survive their massive take off, the flathead's fighting style is short determined runs with the odd bit of head shaking. On light line big ones occasionally act like stingrays and plant themselves on the bottom. When they are close to the boat or shore, I prefer to back the drag off a bit for insurance against their fast take offs. It may take a few more moments to land them but in the long run it pays to be patient.

Big flathead have a certain characteristic to their fight that no other fish in the estuary has and when you feel it a few times you can be sure of the species well before seeing it. They sweep their head from side to side and it feels similar to a tail slowly beating on the line. Little flathead rattle their head about but with big lizards it's more of a slow sweep. The longer each sweep takes, the bigger the flathead.

Flathead don't bite through the line, but they can and do saw through it with rapid head-shakes from side to side. Mostly, but not always, flathead only ever get into serious headshakes when their head cracks the water surface. I believe many so called bite-offs are the result of bad knots rather than toothy lizards. Some anglers automatically reach for a wire trace but this is a bad option as it kills the action of the lure (or bait) and is simply not needed. A short length of line used as a leader, roughly double the strength of the main line is plenty to guard against 'bite offs'.

Big flathead have a fighting style like no other fish.

When they are close to the boat never let their head crack the surface of the water, otherwise they'll go crazy with their headshake routine. It's best to quietly direct them into a waiting landing net rather that risking a straight lift from the water. If you can possibly avoid it, don't use a landing net that is designed for catching prawns as flathead tangle themselves tightly into the mesh and they are incredibly hard to get out.

Once you get to know a waterway you will find that locations with a history of producing quality flathead will keep doing so on a regular basis, even when catch and release is not practiced. This is where local knowledge is very handy and can only be obtained with the use of a fishing guide or by putting in time on the water and remembering exactly where fish were previously caught. The reason a location is a 'hot spot' is often because it is an excellent ambush site with plenty of available food and under these conditions only one or two lizards will be caught. However if it is a breeding site there will be lots of smaller flathead (the males) with only a few large females.

While flathead are a very popular fish, I reckon they are the hardest to handle

An excellent eating sized flathead

without getting spiked. If they are being kept for a feed the safest way of handling them is with a wet rag or towel. You can get a grip on them and the cloth covers the spikes just below the gills, which are the ones that do the most damage. I've been spiked by plenty of flathead and apart from a twitch in the left eye and a slight lisp, (official lie) I'm none the worst for the experience. They bleed a lot and sting a bit but flattie spikes are more of a nuisance than life threatening.

Flathead destined for release should be handled with care. Ideally a pair of long nosed pliers will free the hooks without having to touch the fish but it doesn't always go to plan as they are often hooked deep and they like to thrash about. Holding them with a wet rag so they are upside down (on their back) is the best way I know of to keep them calm. The trouble with the rag is it takes off some of their protective slime, although if the rag is wet the damage should be minimal. I sometimes use my hand to grab them by the bottom jaw while getting the lure out and if done quickly I don't think it hurts them. Jaw grips do not immobilise flathead and you can expect them to have a chew on your thumb. Shop bought jaw clamps work fairly well but they can damage their jaw if you are rough with them.

If you intend to give catch and release a try then it's a good idea to flatten the barbs as it makes the whole operation so much easier. If tension is kept on the line you do not drop fish because of flattened barbs. As there is less bulk, barbless hooks penetrate better, especially if light line is used. The single hook in a soft plastic is a lot easier to get out than treble hooks.

As all large flathead are female, they are the breeding stock of the future and releasing them unharmed is definitely worth a thought. Fish in the crocodile bracket are great to catch but their eating quality is much lower and drier than smaller ones.

I don't begrudge an average angler keeping a once in a lifetime trophy sized flathead because in the overall scheme of things there is very little difference. It's the people who regularly catch and keep the big super breeders who worry me.

A nice flounder on a plastic worm.

LURES

The correct lure choice comes down to the species and size of the fish to be targeted. A good all-round lure is a buoyant diving minnow of roughly 5 to 7cm in length. This size is ideal for bream and also catches a lot of average sized flathead plus the occasional big one. These are the most popular amongst lure fishermen because of their ability to catch both species and there is a better chance of returning with a feed.

To get the most action from a lure it's best to join them to the line either by a loop knot or a swivel and snap. This connection allows more freedom of movement so the lure can perform as designed. If you simply join it with a tight knot the lure will not run at its peak. This is especially important when using small lures. My personal choice is a loop knot, (using a uni knot), as I don't trust a lot of snaps, yet if you are a habitual lure changer a swivel and snap is probably the way to go.

Big flathead are more tempted to strike at a big lure so if you specifically want a big lizard then a diving lure of around 15cm is recommended. Even with a lure this big a surprising amount of average sized flatties are landed. A bonus with using larger lures is the increased possibility of hooking a jew or mangrove jack.

OYSTER LEASES

As far as fish are concerned, oyster leases are a big food barn. They are attracted to these large structures not only for the numerous styles of food, but also for shelter and ambush sites. Oyster leases are also worked by farmers trying to make a living and stealing from them is bad form.

If you are going into a new area I highly recommend doing so on a low tide. That way it's easy to see exactly where the leases are located. Many are badly marked and on a high tide it's easy to get into trouble. The majority of oysters are on timber racks, although there is a swing towards growing them in plastic drums. There are two styles with the drums, floating and sunken. If you are not getting success from lures placed close to the drums, try to hit the drum with the lure and let it sit motionless in the water for a few moments. This is non-retrieve fishing and it's very effective. Bream often sit under the drums and when something crashes into it they expect it to act stunned from the impact. If you don't get a strike while the lure is motionless, a slight twitch of the rod adds life to the lure and increases the chances of a strike. The same style can be used against the outside boards of a fenced lease. If you hit the drum or fence too often bream will wise up and go off the bite.

Flathead don't mind a big plastic. (Photo by M. Phillips)

Bass are a great option in brackish and fresh water.

Most anglers drift with the tide and cast in close to the leases. Many of the leases are set up in lanes, which are ideal for getting deeper into the rough stuff. When you hook a fish in these lanes there is no room for mucking around because you have to get them out fast or they will clean you up. It's not too hard to bullock bream out of these tight spots but big flathead are a different story. If you are drifting and have hooked a fish in a lane there is not much time before the current runs the boat past the lane's entrance. Big flathead give the most problems and if you have an electric motor to hold against the current there is a chance of success, otherwise the fish will be lost. Most luring in estuaries is done on light line but oyster leases are rough country and ideally a heavier line class is used.

An even mixture of bream and flathead can be expected and when fishing with a mate I like to run a 15cm lure targeting big flathead while the other person uses a smaller one for bream. This covers the available options and is generally more productive. Yet if the bream are reasonably thick I'll quickly change. Often bream will follow the larger lure and when this happens I swap to a smaller one and work the water the bream originally came from. Bream lures also catch flathead but larger specimens do prefer a bigger target.

The scar on this bream's head is from a suspected encounter with a net.

When I'm alone I often carry two rods with varying sized rigs attached. For the majority of the time I use the smaller bream lure because they are the most productive. The big lure or plastic is saved for specific locations with a history of quality lizards.

Mangrove jacks are a chance in the Port Macquarie area and the further north you go, the better your chances get.

The most radical style of luring the leases that I've heard of is targeting them when the tide is high. Shallow running or surface lures are cast well over the oysters with a slow retrieve, 10 kilo line and a long strong rod. As soon as a fish hits, they give them nothing, rip back hard keeping the rod held high and wind in quick. Bream are the target and the idea is to keep them high in the water and try to 'plane' them across the surface to the boat. This can be done day or night but it is an acquired skill that doesn't suit everyone. Even with heavy gear lure losses are inevitable, especially when stud bream are on the prowl.

In reality most anglers luring the leases are only scratching the edges. If the lure is put in too far it will probably snag and even if a fish takes it, chances are it will bust the line on oysters. Even so, it can be quite productive.

GOING FOR A FLICK

Casting lures or plastics is an active form of fishing that can be done from the bank, although best results are achieved from a boat, kayaks or canoe. The idea is to put it as close to as many fish as you possibly can and this is done by targeting certain areas. In tight to the bank, around fallen trees and mangroves, oyster leases, rock bars and any feature you think may hold fish. Wharves, moored boats, creek mouths and the edge of a channel are also worth a shot.

For this to be effective you need the right delivery system. A light whippy rod with either a pistol grip or normal butt matched to a small overhead or egg-beater reel. Small minnow lures and light plastics typically used on bream are very light and the rod and reel has to be capable of casting them. The most common fishing line used ranges between 2 and 4 kilo and if the rod loads-up (bends) well with these lines its casting ability should be fine.

Targeting whiting on surface poppers has an enthusiastic following.
(Picture by M. Phillips).

For casting with an overhead I prefer a single-handed pistol grip rod. Little eggbeaters perform best on a light double-handed (standard) rod with a short butt for ease of single handed casting. With overhead and eggbeater reels there is any number of high quality units available, although this is not the case with closed face reels.

I've owned three well-known brands of closed face reels and none could be described as quality units. Their drag system leaves a lot to be desired and the internal pin used to lay line on the spool is prone to wearing. The line wears a groove in the pin, sometimes after only a few outings. When tight line is run through this groove it often breaks, which is the cause of many unexplained bust offs. Generally speaking the more you pay the better the quality and while the targeted species are not overly big, constant casting will soon expose any faults in your gear.

To be really effective anglers need to hunt the fish and think about what they are doing. You will still catch fish by casting all over the place, but not nearly as many as when you put in the effort and use your brain. It's easy to fall into a mechanical mode of cast and retrieve when the fishing is quiet.

This big breeder and just about everything this bloke catches is released.
(Photo by M. Carter)

To fill in time before the next strike it's a good idea to always cast at a target. It may be a leaf, the base of a log or tree, or even a rock on the waters edge. This improves accuracy and keeps your brain as active as your casting arm. It also improves your catch rate. Lure retrieval speed is normally reasonably slow. Most reels are fairly high geared and it's easy to wind a bit fast. Speed by itself is useless in estuaries. The idea is to get the lure working seductively, not radically. Madly twitching the rod tip while retrieving is something I rarely do. It looks impressive on television but in real life I don't think it makes a lot of difference, other than momentarily ruining the action of a neatly running lure. One exception to this is when chasing pike (generally for live bait) because they do tend to get switched on when the lure is acting radical.

While really accurate casting is a handy skill to have, it's not totally necessary. New chums to the sport who have read up on the subject may be under the impression that without pinpoint accuracy they are not in the race. This is simply not the case. Even raw beginners are in with a chance of success and after a few hours of flicking rigs around, you'll be amazed at how accurate you become.

Sooner or later everyone throws an uncharacteristic cast high into a tree and apart from being embarrassing, it's frustrating to see but not be able to reach the snagged lure. In this situation a long-handled landing net makes a great tackle-back as they are often long enough to reach the lure. The netting easily tangles the trebles and allows the angler to pull it out of the timber. The same style can be used on lures snagged under the water line, if the handle is long enough.

After a few hours in a boat, walking the sand flats while flicking out a soft plastic or hard bodied lure is an enjoyable and often productive way to stretch your legs. Flathead are the main target although bream and whiting may also be present. If fishing with kids a stop on the sand flats lets them burn off excess energy and give you a bit of space. Deserted sand flats give a peaceful feeling of being in a remote area, even though civilisation may be just around the corner.

Anglers using paddle power often make the tide work to their advantage. They launch an hour or so before a tidal change which allows them drift with the current while casting close to the bank. When the tide changes they drift back to the starting point. It's amazing what you see while quietly drifting with the tide. A small shower of prawns is a dead give away of a feeding predator and if you can pop a shot close to where the action was then the chance of a strike is excellent. Not all of the 'plop' sounds you hear are falling mangrove seeds as bream make the same sound when they take a crab off the water's edge. Early morning is ideal for this style because there is less chance of wind mucking up your positioning. There is also the safety aspect of no wind chop on the water or rev-heads in ski boats.

I enjoy fishing the early morning period because there is less wind, less heat and everything seems fresh and new. Fish can be caught right through the day yet once the wind picks up it gets a bit harder. When the wind gets up too much casting and boat positioning becomes difficult and if you still need to go fishing then trolling is worth a thought.

TROLLING

Lure trolling is an effective way of covering a lot of water while keeping the lure in the strike zone. It can be done in a paddled canoe or kayak, punt or runabout. With boats I believe an electric motor is the best form of power because it's quiet, yet I've still caught fish while chugging along with a noisy outboard. A lot depends on where you are fishing and how much traffic it experiences. Quiet creeks often shut down bite wise when invaded by an outboard, yet fish in noisier locations don't seem to mind.

In its most basic form, trolling lures is simple. Go for a paddle or a slow drive with some lures out the back. Sooner or later you'll catch fish. Obviously there are better ways than trusting blind faith but you catch my drift.

A quality flathead caught on a spinner bait.

With trolling, most of the fishing skills involved are done by the driver of the craft. They are the ones who direct where the lures go and also choose their speed. Apart from lure choice and cleaning leaves and sticks from the trebles, the passenger needs very little angling skills until they hook something. Trolling is a great way of chucking a line with people who haven't got a clue on fishing as it gives them a far better chance of catching something in a respectable size. Visitors, parents, workmates and kids can all come under this category.

Anglers generally target water that is between one and three metres deep, mainly because that is the depth most lures run. Best results come when the lure is shuffling along the bottom or very close to it. You don't pick up too many fish with lures running mid-water, although trevally don't mind them. Backwater areas away from the main river current are the easiest to fish and there is often large sand and mudflats that are ideal for trolling. Using a sounder should increase the catch, not so much by seeing the fish (although it helps) but knowing the terrain plus water depth and adjusting lure selection and boat direction to suit. Plenty of trollers don't have a sounder and still do well so while it's a nice piece of equipment, a sounder is not a necessity.

If you intend to troll then a tackle-back is a handy item to have on board. A tackle-back retrieves lures snagged on the bottom and pays for itself with the first lure saved. Lures that are trolled run deeper than the same lure used for cast and retrieve. When a lure is snagged you simply slide the tackle-back (tied to a cord) down the line, jiggle it about and hopefully it will grab the lure so you can pull it free. Sometimes the weight of the tackle-back is enough to knock the lure off the snag. I use a Snahu, an Australian brand that has a heavy lead body with a few small chains attached to it. The chains are designed to grab the treble hooks. I consider this brand to be the best I've tried; yet any tackle back is better than none. If you use lures you will lose lures, but with a tackle back the losses aren't nearly as harsh.

The ideal troll speed depends on the lure. It should be reasonably slow but fast enough to get the lure's action working. A lure working correctly should get the rod tip vibrating so rather than trying to pick a certain speed, watch the rod tips and adjust your pace accordingly. When the rod tip goes dead you are either going too slow or the lure is fouled with a leaf or stick.

Some anglers swear by trolling with the current because flathead lie facing the tidal flow as they wait for a feed. This theory is fine when the current isn't too strong but once it gets a good pace up you have to drive quite fast to get the lure working correctly. I've trolled against the tide when it's running hard and caught some good fish while doing so.

There are a number of reasons why the rod should be hand held rather than put in a holder while trolling. You can get the lure deeper by lowering the rod tip and with a finger on the line you get a far better indication of what is happening to your lure. You can also strike at any suspect bumps and it keeps passengers occupied.

I reckon the best reason for holding the rod is to get that fantastic energy charge the moment you hook-up to a fish. The rod thumps into life and if it's taking line the charge keeps blasting. It's a feeling I never get sick of. Rods left in a holder can give you a shock when they buckle over, but nothing beats feeling it as well.

This giant herring was caught in the Nambucca River, a rare catch for the area. (Photo by M.Phillips)

BY-CATCH

While bream and flathead are the most common, they are not the only fish caught. Not so long ago whiting on lures was almost unheard of yet now they are a fairly regular capture, especially when small surface poppers or little crawdad lures are used. Luderick, commonly known as blackfish are another fish that show a liking for small crawdads, possibly because they are pink nipper imitations.

Other species that fall to lures include long tom, trevally, tailor, Moses perch plus the occasional Jew. Mangrove jack are a viable option north of Port Macquarie and the closer you get to Brisbane the number of species increases.

CONCLUSION

I enjoy the hunting aspect of using artificial 'baits'. Being physically and mentally active while tossing lures or plastics keeps you involved and interested.

Technological improvements in lure designs, rods, reels and fishing lines have allowed new styles to emerge. I'm not one to race out and try every new gimmick on the market, but I do watch to see which things are working. If they do seem to be successful and they fit into my impression of a good idea, then I'll give them a run.

I remember the first time I figured out how to use 'suspending' minnows. These are basically hard body diving minnows for bass and bream. When you stop retrieving, they stay at the same depth rather than quickly float to the surface. If you cast them close to a deep bank and give it a quick stab with the rod, the lure dives down about half a metre and stays there. It's fished the same as the non-retrieve method with surface lures. Give it the occasional slight twitch to make it look alive and your lure is below the surface in tight to the strike zone a lot longer and it works a treat. Other anglers would have known about it for years, but discovering styles and systems for yourself is very satisfying.

The more you think about, and practice tossing lures and plastics, the better you get. It's not hard to be successful and it's a great way to spend a few hours in the estuary.

BREAM

Bream thrive in a huge range of environments and can be found up creeks in brackish water, down through the rivers and bays, along beaches and ocean rocks and out on many of the close reefs in the ocean. They are often the first fish a kid catches and some anglers stay bream fanatics for a lifetime.

I love catching bream and for as long as I can remember I've always been a bream nut. They are a species that really keep you on your toes with their variety of biting styles. Sometimes they are extremely finicky and almost impossible to hook. Other times they simply pick up the bait, swallow it and keep cruising. There are no taps on the rod tip, it just bends over and you are hooked up. A lot depends on the amount of competition from other fish. It's easy in quiet, calm water for a lone bream to nudge, nip and play around with bait but with a few more fish in the equation, that bait will be quickly eaten.

This bream was caught a fair way out in the ocean at Woody Head.

Anyone who can regularly catch bream in all their habitats on the wide range of styles available would have to be considered a very good angler. This sounds pretty easy until you consider using plastics, diving lures, surface lures, fly fishing plus baits. There is calm water, fast water, deep and shallow water plus areas with a lot of traffic and quiet backwaters. All of these styles have their little tricks, plus the water conditions you are chasing them in force you to vary your approach to be successful.

DRIFTING THE WALL

In autumn and winter, bream move towards the river mouth to breed. During this time their mind is on other things and when they see an opportunity for an easy feed they grab it.

Most rivers run to the ocean between man-made training walls made of rock, commonly called breakwalls. While this section is targeted at walls close to the ocean, I know the same style works along rocky shorelines kilometres from the ocean. It's pretty simple yet extremely effective on bream. You drift along the wall with the current and cast un-weighted baits towards the wall so they slowly sink down close to the rocks.

An excellent fish on the run out tide.

If the tide is rising I like to motor really close towards the ocean end of the wall and let the current push me back up river. This is the only time you get to fish this part of the river because on other tides it's too dangerous.

When the tide is running out I start well upriver and work my way towards the mouth. Always give yourself plenty of time to get organized and the motor running when drifting towards the bar (river mouth) because if anything is going to go wrong, this is where it will happen. The last thing you need is to get swept into dangerous water. If the motor fails, get the anchor out quick and give it plenty of rope so it has a better chance of grabbing. By leaving early a lot of stress can be avoided.

An electric motor used to position the boat is ideal, yet you can get away with using the outboard, a paddle or an oar. Early morning is best because there is generally no wind which makes the system so much easier. There are also less anchored boats in your way. Walls that only have boat access are the best as they will have less people fishing from them. Early morning and late afternoon is generally the best fishing time, but winter bream can often be caught right through the day.

There are two types of bream you can catch, river bream and ocean run bream. River bream are a darker bronzy colour so they blend in better with coloured water and mud or gravel bottoms. Ocean run bream are silvery

45

white in colour to blend in with clean water and a sand bottom. They are both bream, just from a different environment.

Drifting the wall can produce stud bream.

Calm conditions, an electric motor and a breakwall add up to good bream fishing.

Apart from their colour the main difference between the two is their numbers. Bronzy bream are often quality fish but scattered and not in big numbers. Ocean run bream that have just moved into a river can still be found in schools of a few hundred fish, all hungry and competing for food.

I've been lucky enough to find a few of these schools and the fishing is awesome. Stud bream to 40cm were hammering baits within seconds of it hitting the water. The action was so hot I had to change my style of hooking them to prolong the enjoyment. Instead of giving them time to get the bait down, I was striking very early, trying to lip hook them. It didn't matter if I missed because they were almost lined up to belt any scrap left on the hook. The only fish I kept were those deeply hooked and I still had to leave them on the bite. This has happened on a number of occasions over the last few years, yet not nearly enough times to get blasé about it. I know these were special times.

During winter, bream can often be caught right through the day.

Most drifting sessions I go on I get 4 or 5 keepers over 30cm, and sometimes the only ones I keep are deeply hooked. Drifting the wall is a far better way to find the bigger bream. Years ago when I anchored close to the wall we still caught bream and a few good ones as well but when compared to drifting we weren't in the race.

BAIT

All the usual bream baits work, although my favourites are small strip baits of tuna, mullet and sergeant baker, preferably fresh. I do a reasonable amount of offshore fishing and 'bakers' are a by-catch when bottom fishing. They are generally released, but are sometimes used for bait while chasing snapper.

When keeping sergeant baker (or mullet) for bait I scale them then freeze them whole. With the scales removed it is far easier to bait the hook without squashing and damaging the flesh and you don't end up with scales on the hook point.

A good feed of breakwall bream.

When baiting up for bream I've found strip baits work best when you put the hook point first through the flesh and out the skin then turn the hook and push it back through the skin and out the flesh. The baits are roughly 50mm or 2 inches long and about 20mm wide. This gives a bite-sized bait they can easily swallow. Occasionally I flick out bait twice this size to see if it draws in the bigger fish, and sometimes it works.

Overcast days are ideal for bream.

Pink nippers are excellent bait and bream love them, plus they have the added bonus of attracting luderick (blackfish) as well. Because they are so light, a small running sinker is often needed for casting distance.

The same style of drifting the wall using soft plastics instead of bait can be very productive as well.

BREAKWALL RIGS

As you are fishing close to the rocks the rig needs to be simple. A 1/0 hook tied straight to the main line is what I've been using for the last few years. Originally I slipped on a tiny running ball sinker before tying on the hook but I've found it's only needed when the wind is blowing. Flesh baits have enough weight for good casting and they also sink well enough by themselves.

Fishing close to the wall is a trade off, the closer you work the more snags you catch, but you also tend to find the bigger fish.

Smallish eggbeater reels loaded with 3 or 4kg line cast well when matched with a light action rod of about 6 foot or 2 metres. I prefer to run mono line rather than braid for this style. It is cheaper and you do lose a bit of line at times. Apart from the cost, braid often comes in bright colours that really stand out in the clear water of a run up tide.

OCEAN ROCK BREAM

Fishing for bream from the ocean rocks is probably the easiest form of rock fishing available. Done correctly it is great fun and is often a 'stepping stone' toward other more glamorous styles of rock fishing.

Early morning, simple gear and a nice fish

Safety is the number one requirement because the dangers involved are very real. Every year people lose their lives and not all of them were fishing at the time. The ocean in all its moods is a dangerous thing. When taken lightly it tends to come back at you very hard.

Don't take your kids rock fishing until you have sufficient experience and they are mature enough to do so with safety. My dad didn't have a clue about fishing but one of his mates was an experienced rock fisherman and he taught me when I was about 8 years old. All of these years later I'm still grateful because it is still one of my favorite forms of fishing.

A good rock fisherman always watches the water and reacts to what it is doing. When tying on a hook, rebaiting or getting a drink, get into

49

the habit of always facing the water so you can still watch how it is acting.

Low light periods such as early morning, late afternoon or dull overcast days are ideal times to chase bream. Some locations loose the sun quite early in the afternoon due to large headlands and cliff faces. Often these places fire up early because the sun is off the water. While low light levels are preferred it's fairly common to pick them up at any time of day, which definitely adds to their appeal.

For most rock fisherman it's more of a package deal rather than simply a tunnelled vision attempt to harvest bream. The whole environment gets you in. Daybreak is a magical time to be perched on a rock next to the ocean. More often than not a pod of dolphins will cruise past as they patrol the edge of

A good bream off the rocks.

the white water and sometimes they really get carried away riding waves and jumping about. Quite often I'll go chasing bream because I feel like it, not necessarily because it's a great time to go, yet I generally get a few and that satisfies me. Even the times I get skunked and don't catch anything it's no big deal, unless it happens too often.

Most of the locations I fish work better on a rising tide and once the tide changes the tempo tends to taper off. Although not all spots are the same as some locations fish much better on a falling tide, so it pays to get your area wired by putting in the time.

Along the north coast autumn and winter are the most productive times for ocean rock bream with a high percentage of fish being males. Many locals regard Anzac Day as the start of the season but there is no real starting or finishing date when it comes to bream. However what does happen is the mullet start their spawning run to sea in autumn when the winds have a fair bit of south westerly in them. When the mullet start to run, good numbers of bream soon follow.

No matter where you find them, bream are always a challenge to hook. In the turbulent environment off the ocean rocks they simply don't have time to be too suspicious of a bait. Although most cases you have to concentrate and show some skill to hook them.

Every time you go after them their bite is slightly different. This keeps interest levels high and also does quite a bit for your angling skills. Plenty of the top rock fishermen who are now successful on jew, tuna and even marlin learned their skills on bream and plenty still chase them when the big fish don't want to play.

It pays to remember that bream have a small mouth and this has a direct

relationship with the way they take a bait. Big aggressive bream can swallow the bait on their first bite making a hook-up as simple as leaning back on the rod. Yet bream mostly bump or tap the bait a few times before you can hook solid weight. If you strike too early then chances are you've blown it. Unless there are big numbers around, it's generally only the

Fresh from the water they are a beautiful fish.

little ones come back for a second try after the fright of being struck at. It's more productive to wind in, put on a presentable bait and cast it to where you want it rather than to wait with suspect bait in the hope the fish will come back.

When a bream bumps my bait I generally lower the rod tip and swing it towards the fish. This gives a little bit of loose line so the bream doesn't feel any resistance. Normally there are another one or two bumps before a solid take. I feel the line, watch the line and watch the rod tip while still keeping an eye on the water. The strike is made as the rod starts to load up on weight. This style gives an excellent hook-up ratio and tends to hook them in the mouth instead of down deep in their gills or gut.

From the first bump to the stage where you lift them out of the water takes concentration and can be distracting, but it is important to never forget to keep an eye on the water. Seasoned rock fishermen constantly watch for incoming waves whether they are hooked up or not as it becomes second nature. Yet new chums and even occasional rock fishermen tend to forget where they are when concentrating on a fish.

The common statement of 'a wave popped up out of no-where and soaked me' would be more accurate if said as 'I didn't see the wave coming and got soaked.' Waves don't just 'pop up' 2 or 3 metres off the rocks. They roll in from out wide and it's not always the really big ones you have to worry about. Quite often (but not always) big waves roll over and break well out from the rocks, losing much of their power in the process. Under these conditions it's the small to medium sized waves that can catch you off guard. They have a habit of holding up, continually building in size until they roll over and dump directly onto the shore.

Always go with a partner as it is far safer and a lot more fun. If one person does fall in, the other should not blindly jump in after them. All that achieves is two people in the water instead of one.

A late afternoon, sea-run bream.

The easiest way to see if a location is safe to fish is to take your time and watch the water and wave patterns, preferably from a high vantage point before you start fishing. If there is any doubt then give it a miss and find somewhere more sheltered. If it looks okay then go down and put your backpack, bucket or tackle box etc onto a high ledge where there is no chance of it getting wet from the waves. There's no need to cart a heap of junk to the actual rock you are fishing off as it gets in the way.

When looking for a ledge or boulder to fish from there are a number of things to consider. Safety is obviously the number one consideration because you're not there to put your life on the line. Where-ever possible I prefer a reasonably flat dry ledge that drops straight down to the water as it's easier to land fish by lifting them straight out rather than bumping them up a sloping rock-face. These ledges are not always available over good bream water and there will be times you have to improvise and put up with uncomfortable rock formations. A simple thing to remember is that if you are standing on a wet rock there is an excellent chance you will also get wet. So for safety and the sake of comfort, I nearly always fish from a dry rock and rarely get my feet wet.

BREAM WATER

Bream are mostly found in turbulent aerated white water reasonably close to the rocks. Areas such as small bays and gutters are ideal, especially if they have a bit of depth and plenty of active water. Bream like white water because it supplies them with food washed from the rocks plus a certain degree of safety, which are two basic requirements for survival.

Big bream make the cold weather worth it.

In most situations there is no need for long distance casting as most of the action is in close. Features are the main things to look for as these tend to attract and hold fish. A deep hole or gutter with a good coverage of white water is ideal, as are areas where a good wash is working. For those new to the game a 'wash' is created after a wave has broken on the shore and boils back into the ocean. It's a big plume of white water filled with air bubbles pushing out into clear water.

Areas where finger shaped rock formations push out into the ocean are ideal for bream. Most people tend to walk to the end of the fingers and cast out wide, but a better idea is to fish the turbulent water in the gutter between the fingers. When a school of bream moves in the action can be fast and furious and with a constant burley flow they stick around for a fair amount of time. The down side to working these gutters is you are often standing side-on to the waves and it's easy to forget to keep an eye on the ocean while you are watching your line.

Occasionally you will find the need to throw a long cast but again it should be directed at a feature rather than just for the sake of it. When a fair casting distance is required the usual rig is a reasonable sized lead on the reel side of a swivel with roughly half a metre of line to the hook.

Being flexible enough to compromise and try something different can often

Winter bream are generally good fish.

be the difference between a good outing and a bad one. There are plenty of 'rules' for getting the best results, yet most of them need to be moulded to suit the conditions.

Bream are quite often found under a working school of tailor, feeding on the scraps that sink to the bottom. When the tailor go off the bite, it's a great time to target bream because there should still be plenty of scraps in the water and bream will hang around to clean it up. Fresh strip baits of tailor are excellent on bream and fresh tailor gut is even better.

BAITS

Bream have a wide ranging diet as they are both a scavenger and a predator. Oily flesh baits such as tuna cubes, pilchard pieces or mullet strips are ideal because they put the smell or taste into the water which helps bream hunt them down.

Offal baits such as mullet gut, chicken gut and tailor gut are also extremely effective because they release heaps of juices and small particles into the water. Gut baits lose their effectiveness when they start to look anaemic and washed out, so when this happens, change it for a fresh one and throw the scraps into the water for burley.

My favourite bream baits for off the rocks are either small mullet strips or chicken gut. Both stay on the hook quite well and fish have to work pretty hard to get them off. They are also robust enough to stay on the hook when being battered about by rough water. Bream will also take prawns, pipis, bread, crabs, nippers and worms, plus off-beat baits such as cheese, liver and strips of chicken breast.

A common mistake is to over-crowd the hook with a bait that is too large. This tends to force bream to pick at it until it is small enough for them to swallow. The hook point should always be showing and with strip baits be careful that skin cannot foul the point of the hook. I like a strip bait to be slightly longer than the hook as this gives the fish a tempting bite-sized feed. The hook is pushed through the bait on the flesh side then reversed back through the skin, leaving the point showing on the flesh side. If the flesh is too thick then trim it to size before you put it on the hook.

His first bream for the morning, well above legal.

ROCK FISHING RIGS

The two major bream rigs used off the rocks are either a small ball sinker running directly to the hook, or a swivel roughly half a metre from the hook with a running sinker on the angler side of the swivel. I use a 1/0 size hook and it's about as big as you would want to go. Smaller hooks will also catch bream and if prawns are your preferred bait then a long shank hook will present the bait better.

Most anglers use 4 to 6kg line due to the harsh conditions being fished. 6kg does seem heavy for bream but it is handy for pulling rigs off snags or when there is a lot of loose weed in the water.

A nice fish caught anchored within one kilometre of a river mouth.

CONCLUSION

I really enjoy the simplicity of catching bream off the rocks. You travel lightly which is a refreshing change when compared to the amount of junk carried in while targeting larger fish. The ocean rocks are a wild untamed place and chasing bream gives you a great reason to be there.

DRUMMER

Drummer are found well south of Sydney with numbers tapering off around Brisbane. For sheer brute strength and explosive dirty tactics the drummer is hard to beat. Found around the ocean rocks in reasonable numbers, drummer, both silver and black; grow to around 9 kilo and 75cm in length, with an average fish weighing in at one to two kilo. While small ones obviously exist, in many areas drummer are rarely caught under one kilo.

For the sake of simplicity and to save on duplication I have joined the silver drummer and black drummer together in this chapter. In actual fact the black drummer is not a drummer at all. Its correct name is eastern rock blackfish which is a totally different family to that of the drummer. Yet for all intents and purposes the angling skills needed for both of these species is the same. They both fight extremely hard and dirty; they take the same baits, look similar and are found in the same environment.

The main difference I have found is the eastern rock blackfish (black drummer) is slightly darker and has 13 dorsal fin spines and has whiter flesh that is not as course. The silver drummer is slightly lighter coloured and has 11 dorsal fin spines.

Many anglers simply call them pigs because they are so fat, and unless you are right into competition fishing where there are points for different species, or you are chasing a record, there is not a great deal to be gained from picking the differences, except for personal satisfaction.

BAITS AND BURLEY

The drummer's habitat is extremely close to the rocky shoreline amongst aerated white water. An inspection of their stomach contents typically shows a dominance of brown weed with a bit of green weed and shell grit.

Landing one of these certainly puts you in a good mood.

While they are commonly classified as weed eaters, drummer also feed on flesh baits such as cunje, prawns, pink nippers and crabs. Strange as it sounds, adding minced pilchards or tuna oil to a bread based burley also has the effect of bringing them on the bite and holding them in the area for longer, so they are far from strict vegetarians.

Bread, affectionately known as white cunje, is excellent drummer bait. Fresh sliced white bread gives the best results, probably because it is the easiest to mould around the hook. Bait presentation suffers once the bread goes stale so try to keep the loaf in shade while you are out on the rocks.

While some anglers like to use the crust, most find the softer centre part easier to put on a hook. Each slice gives two good drummer baits, which is excellent value when the cost of bread is considered.

Bread is surprisingly tough bait that withstands attack from 'rubbish' fish much better than the more traditional baits such as prawn or cunje. The hard smooth surface of a good bread bait means that 'pickers' have a problem getting a purchase point to rip open the bait. Bread is not immune to attack from pickers, but it is tough enough to allow you to successfully continue fishing when large schools of 'rubbish' fish have been burleyed up.

Drummer definitely like bread and it's the best bait I know of for getting around the pickers. Yet for me its greatest attraction is the fact that it's totally foreign bait. Nothing is taken from the ocean to produce bread so you are actually adding to the eco-system you are fishing. The more traditional baits of cunje or prawns by their very nature have to be plundered from the ocean.

A 2kg drummer caught on fresh white bread.

Cunje is gathered during calm weather on a low tide, sometimes a few days before a planned fishing trip. It's often said that you can't beat fresh local bait but this is not always the case. One time that springs to mind where local bait didn't work was one occasion while drummer fishing with a few mates. The seas were fairly calm and there wasn't much white water. Predictably, fishing was quite slow. As it was low tide my mates decided to collect some cunje and they were a bit surprised when I declined and told them I'd stick to the white stuff.

They collected enough cunje for 10 or so baits each. With ultra fresh bait they fished with a new sense of enthusiasm but the rewards didn't come. Sweep and other small fish moved in and demolished their baits with regular monotony. We caught three drummer that morning, all on bread.

In hindsight the cunje taken from the rocks didn't serve any purpose and was basically wasted. It could be argued, and rightfully so, that cunje is a top bait and these blokes were thinking anglers who took the initiative by gathering fresh bait when the opportunity was presented.

Fresh out of the water they are very hard to hold.

Yet at the end of the day all that was achieved was a slight dent in the drummer's preferred environment by the loss of that cunje. It's true that future storms may well have ripped those cunje off the rocks leaving a similar result, but nature does what it wants and you can't change that. However given a good alternative such as bread, we can limit the negative impact on the environment we fish.

On a serious drummer outing I generally stuff about 3 loaves of bread into my backpack for burley, plus I buy a fresh loaf on the way for bait. This is enough to keep a constant trickle going into the water for about 3 or more hours. The trick with burley is to use a little bit often. The bread should be soaked and thoroughly mashed in water. If too much water is in the burley bucket it's much harder to properly mash the bread, resulting in larger pieces floating away on the surface. This floating burley is wasted as it generally feeds seagulls, not drummer.

BREAD BAITS

Fold the slice in half and neatly tear the bread away from the crust, getting as much in one piece as possible. Once the crust is gone (into the burley if it is soft), keep it folded and tear it in half so you have two folded squares.

Place the hook on top of the square and wrap the bread around the hook, moulding it as you go. The idea is to have a hard teardrop shaped cylinder of bread dough with only the hint of a hook point showing.

Fresh bread is easy to mould around a hook and as long as you squash it in nice and tight you can't go too far wrong. As there is very little hook point showing these baits can be worked over incredibly rough country without instantly snagging the bottom. This is an important trait when the drummers preferred environment is considered because they really do love the rough stuff.

Bread, prawns, cunje and weed are all good drummer baits.

Sometimes you can get a loaf of bread that has a really tough crust all the way around it. These are generally found at a bakery, or the cheap supermarket stuff. These crusts are so hard you can tear a length of the slice and hook it up like a strip bait. Loaves like these provide a huge number of baits.

DRUMMER WATER

Areas with plenty of aerated white water working over reasonably deep reefs and sunken boulders covered in weed growth are ideal for drummer. Places where waves are hammering into weedy rock faces are also productive as the fish feed on the dislodged weed, shellfish and crabs. Small rocky bays and gutters are almost guaranteed action as long as there is enough turbulence in the water. Sandy bottomed depressions surrounded by weedy rock faces are also excellent drummer holes. I've also had good success on breakwalls that have a bit of wave action as well.

Overcast days with a bit of swell are ideal.

White water is a major key to success on drummer as they go quiet when the ocean is glassed out. This does not mean you have to fish extremely wild water to catch them, as that attitude will often put you in danger. Over the years I've caught plenty from water that was reasonably stable. The trick is to target where there is white water working. It may only be a small patch of white water and you will probably need to work your bait very close to the rocks, but that's the best place to find them. They are also found around offshore islands and bomboras in the same water conditions described above. Much of the north coast's inter-tidal zone is steep and in many respects

quite barren. Compared to further south there are very few beds of cabbage weed and the rock pools don't seem to hold nearly as much marine life. I don't believe this is due to over exploitation by humans, which has been a problem in other areas. I think it's more a climatic difference combined with a steep intertidal zone that is often too harsh for weed to grow. Weed also tends to grow better on sandstone rather than volcanic rock. Add to this an uncountable tonnage of shifting sand as it works its way up the coast and a grim picture could be painted. Yet it's not grim as there are some nice fish landed off these rocks.

Sandstone ledges, Alvey reels and drummer go hand in hand. (Photo by B. Osborne)

Because you are fishing right in close to the rough stuff, getting snagged (hooked on the bottom) has to happen occasionally. When you feel a snag, try jiggling and bouncing the rod tip before you put solid pressure on the line. With practice you'll be able to get the hook off a lot of snags. If you can't get it off, the line needs to be broken. The best way to break it is wind up any slack line, make sure the rod is pointing at the snag, hold the spool so it doesn't slip, and start walking in the opposite direction. The line will stretch and then break. If you can't break it, you are fishing with line that is too heavy for you.

THE BITE

Quite often the first sign of a bite is a few deceptively light bumps felt through the line a fraction of a second before a huge surging run. If you have too much slack line then you will not feel the light bumps and the first sign of a bite will be instant massive weight.

Things happen really quickly when they feel the hook. I've seen a mate hook up and be blown away before he even knew he had a bite! What happened was that his line was drifting close to the rock wall and out to his right with the current, when all of a sudden the line raced out to his left and into a deep crevice. He didn't see it as he was watching an incoming wave and he didn't notice anything through the line. When I pointed to the line he thought he was simply snagged, but the speed his line raced against the current and where it ended up meant that for my money it had to be a drummer.

Because of their brutal fighting style the best way to hold the rod is with the butt firmly against your lower hip. This way you are prepared to fight the fish the instant you hook-up. If for example you are holding the rod butt under the armpit, you lose the advantage of leverage and by the time you wrestle it into a fighting position, the drummer will most likely have found sanctuary in a rock crevice or under a ledge. Either way the fish will most likely win because

A mixed bag and the reel used to catch them.

if you give them half a chance they'll beat you. One way to keep control of loose line is to slowly wind in once the bait has sunk. A lot of drummer fishermen use this style all the time, but I prefer to follow the bait with the rod tip and pick up loose line only when necessary. The use of light lead on heavy line will always result in some loose line in the system; the trick is to keep it to a minimum.

Given half a chance most drummer will go for broke, running deep into cover. This generally results in an instant bust off as the line rubs through on rock. Sometimes the line doesn't break but you still can't get the fish out. Drummer often crash dive into holes and erect their dorsal fins. These fins are made up of solid stumpy spines which effectively jambs them in there, making it impossible to pull them out. When the fish decides it is safe to come out they relax their spines and simply back out. I've 'swum' drummer out of a crevice by using patience and no tension on the line, yet it's very hard to tell if you are connected to a fish or the hook has came out and you are snagged.

Drummer still have plenty of strength left when you pull them out of the water and for the inexperienced, they can be a real handful. They are fairly slippery and while they don't have many spikes, it's common for them to draw blood from the angler when given room to thrash about. Often the spines along their back line do the damage, but the plate around their gills is also sharp enough to cut, especially when your fingers are wet and soft. The easiest way I've found to control drummer is to hold them upside down and securely tuck them under your arm like a football. This points their spines away from your body, plus any fish held upside down tends to be much calmer. It's a good way to hold them while taking the hook out.

BEST TIME

Winter and early spring are the best time of year to target them because the water temperature is generally lower and this is when they tend to feed most on baits other than weed. Water temperatures of 17 degrees Celsius and lower are ideal. Many anglers believe them to be a purely winter species but this is not completely true. While cold water definitely helps with catching numbers, they can be caught all year round. It's rare to find summer drummer in a feeding frenzy, but they are about and if one or two fish are enough to classify the outing as a success then you shouldn't have too many bad days during the warmer months. I've caught these 'winter fish' in February when the water was 25 degrees and offshore anglers were hooking into Spanish mackerel.

Peak feeding times vary between locations, mainly due to how the wave action is working against the rocks. Some places fire up at low tide because this is when the water is shallowest and waves are thumping directly into weed covered rocks, breaking off more food than when the tide is high and the waves are using most of their energy to batter barren rock. Other locations fire best on high tide where the waves are able to reach into beds of cabbage weed, dislodging plenty of food in the process. A lot of anglers believe a rising tide to be the best.

BUTTERFISH

Butterfish, sometimes known as bat fish, are a real problem on the north coast. They are aggressive feeders capable of tearing most baits apart within moments of splash down. Burley quickly brings them out of the woodwork and if you feed them enough it's not uncommon to have them literally boil

Heavy line is needed to pull drummer away from the snags. (Photo by B. Osborne)

on the water surface in their frantic feeding frenzy. South West Rocks is generally the southern-most point where butterfish are a problem. They are also found further south but as yet not in plague proportions.

When butterfish or other 'rubbish' fish are in the area burleying is basically a waste of time because it brings too many in. Yet if you must persist with burley, bread baits with a reasonably heavy lead are one way of getting past most of them. The lead sends the bait down quickly into the strike zone, past the majority of butterfish that are feeding on burley in the top layer of water. Even so, when butterfish are thick you will still have to replace your bread baits every few minutes but at least you can still continue fishing.

Butterfish don't seem to like water temperatures under 20 degrees Celsius so they aren't a real problem during most of the winter months. Yet every year they seem to become more acclimatised and it wouldn't surprise me if in 10 or more years they were around for the full 12 months.

DRUMMER GEAR

While they can be caught on a wide range of gear including eggbeaters and overheads, an Alvey reel matched to a fairly long, strong rod with a soft tip and a short butt is the best way to go. Alveys are unbeatable when it comes to pure winching power, which is a big plus when the drummer's dirty tactics are considered.

15 kilo is the preferred line class used by many experienced drummer anglers. This may sound like it is too heavy but even when fished aggressively with a hard drag there are no guarantees. I've been blown away by big drummer using 15 kilo line and never looked like winning the battle. One memorable time I was busted up three times in a row. As fast as I could get a bait in the water I was being blown away. The next bite I struck hard like the last ones, but instead of being dragged toward the edge of the rocks, I launched a bream of almost one kilo onto the rocks behind me. I felt like real dill, and probably was, but it does show how hard you have to fight big drummer in rough country to be in with a chance.

Obviously if you are not physically capable of fishing 15 kg hard then there is very little sense in using it and dropping down to 10 kg line would be a smart move. Unless you are constantly catching small fish, anything lighter than 10 kilo on drummer is asking for trouble.

As heavy line and an aggressive attitude are used to battle them, the hook needs to be very strong. Ideally a 1/0 Mustad 542 hook should be used, otherwise any extra strong 1/0 will do the job. I often fish with a pea-sized sinker running straight to the hook and let the bait wash around with the current, yet other anglers prefer a heavier ball sinker to stop the bait moving too much and finding a snag.

Lead selection really depends on the amount of water movement on the day. If the water is really turbulent with a solid drift and a tiny sinker is used, chances are the bait will continually surge around near the surface, which is a sign you are not fishing with enough weight. Some anglers use float rigs similar to those for luderick, only beefed up considerably.

Got to be happy with a nice drummer.

LIGHT LINE DRUMMER

These are extremely powerful, dirty fighters and in most situations light line gives no chance of landing the fish. Yet it is possible if the right location is chosen.

I'd always envied luderick anglers who accidentally hooked a drummer on light gear yet still managed to land it. I figured the fight would be awesome (and it is) and they would stretch you to the limit. Although the idea of continually being busted up and leaving hooks in fish didn't sit too well with my idea of fair play. It took me a number of years before trying light line on drummer because it took a fair while to figure out how to do it and then be confident enough to try it.

Choosing the right location is the key to success on light line drummer. Generally you would be looking for an area with a good wash with plenty of underwater features covered in cunje and weed. Yet for light line these sorts of places are hopeless, as the fish will beat you virtually every time.

Kids need to be strong, capable anglers before tackling drummer.
Photo by D. Clarke

What you should look for is a location with a clean sandy bottom that runs right to the base of the rocks. Ideally it should have a fair depth with plenty of weed growth and white aerated water working along the edge. I prefer the rock ledge to drop straight down into the depths, as these cutaway ledges tend to have fewer places for drummer to smash you off. Also if the drop-off is at your feet you can hold the rod out wide, which is extremely handy when a rampaging drummer is running in tight along the wall. If there is a bed of cabbage weed beside this clean water drummer site then the chances are excellent of finding fish because with the right seas it will become a natural burley pot.

Last but not least, the location should have a spot where you can wash the fish out. They are often around 2 kilos and trying to lift a thrashing fish of this size on light line is fraught with danger. Washing a fish out is a great skill to learn. Basically what you do is use the waves to wash the fish up onto a ledge, wait for another swell to wash it a bit higher and keep doing this until it is safe to go get it. Things get complicated when the fish doesn't stay on the ledge and washes back with the outgoing surge. You have to give it line as you follow it with the rod tip because if you try to bullock it around, the light line will break. If you cannot see a way of landing a drummer from a likely looking spot then don't work it with light gear.

A nice little summer drummer.

These clean water conditions described are not the drummer's natural environment and unless burley is used, the only chance of scoring a hit is from the odd travelling fish. Even with burley it would be an extremely optimistic angler who thought he could hold a school of fish for any length of time.

Under these conditions I prefer a long rod to hold the line out from the rocks and to help soak up the hammering dished out from a good fish. It is also useful when directing fish away from danger areas with sideways pressure.

When fishing light I use a 4 metre beach rod and an Alvey loaded with 6 kilo line. This line class may not sound very light but unless you choose your site well, your chances of winning the battle are slim.

If deeply hooked, drummer have the dentistry to quickly chew through fishing line so I tend to strike them fairly early. For added insurance with light line, either a short doubled main line using a spider hitch or a short leader of 15 kilo tied with a double uni knot is used. With these rigs the lead runs directly to the hook. If using an Alvey and a fair casting distance is involved, a swivel joining the leader to the main line will help stop line twist.

CATCH AND RELEASE

These fish are an excellent proposition for catch and release fishing. The fight is short and brutal and you either land them quickly or they bust you off. This means that on capture they are still fit and healthy, giving an excellent survival rate when released.

One common grumble with catch and release is that you are letting the fish go; only to be netted by the pros at a later date. This does not apply to drummer as they are one of the few species professional fisherman do not target. So if their numbers decline, the blame will land squarely on the shoulders of recreational fisherman.

They are also said to be a slow growing fish that live for a long time.

Drummer are great fish for catch and release. (Photo by D. Clarke)

Given the fact these fish are only average table fare, plus they are still extremely healthy when landed, it makes them an obvious choice for catch and release. To my way of thinking their greatest asset is their size and reasonably easy accessibility. These days regularly catching fish well over one kilo from the rocks is not that easy, although with drummer it's still possible.

Thinking anglers have been limiting their catch for years by keeping the blood lust to a minimum and only taking a feed. The old idea of proving your angling skills by killing every legal sized fish caught is thankfully changing to a more conservative approach. Yet for many anglers the idea of releasing a 2 kilo plus fish is still a novelty. It's ok to keep a few for the table but when the opportunity arises, give catch and release a try. The thrill of the capture is the draw card and releasing them unharmed is the icing on the cake.

CONCLUSION

For pure raw power there aren't many fish rougher or tougher than drummer. They put up a massive fight on light gear and if you target them with the wrong gear or in the wrong place, the battle will be over in the blink of an eye.

A big, fat healthy drummer (Picture by D. Clarke)

GETTING OFFSHORE WITHOUT A BOAT

The easiest way to go offshore fishing is to book a trip on a charter boat. It's also a great way to find out if you like offshore fishing. They supply all the gear and bait needed, plus many have coffee and light refreshments as well. Apart from the boat, the greatest thing they have is an excellent local knowledge on the best spots and what is available at that time of year. If you are happy to go offshore 3 or 4 times a year then charters are better options, money wise, than owning an offshore boat. When you think about boat and trailer rego, keeping up to date with safety equipment and keeping the rig maintained to a high enough standard to safely run outside, it's getting expensive. Then you have fuel, bait, all the fishing gear needed plus fishing and boat licence. On top of all that is the necessity of a tow vehicle, probably a 4WD big enough to get your boat to and from the ramp. All of these costs are after buying the boat.

Owning an offshore boat and keeping it well maintained is a surprisingly expensive exercise. Many simply can't afford it and for a lot of years I was

Charter boats know how to put you onto fish.

also in this position, yet I still managed to go offshore on a regular basis. Just about every boat owner needs a companion to fish with, preferably someone who can lend a hand with anchoring, netting or gaffing fish, plus launching and retrieving the boat. These helpers are called deckies, which are basically people who sometimes kick in a bit for fuel, or just get a free ride and hopefully work for their passage.

The best way to find a skipper in need of a deckie is to join an offshore fishing club. These are people who actually go fishing, not the ones who talk it up in the pub but rarely get their boat wet. This is how I got my start. Go to the meetings, weigh-ins and BBQ's and let it be known that you are available and keen to get outside. Sooner or later someone will give you a run and if you are compatible with the skipper there is a good chance it will become a regular event. Plenty of boat owners have trouble finding someone who is reliable and available, often at short notice.

The quickest way of losing the privilege is to run down the skipper's boat handling or fishing abilities behind his back, because they will find out. If you believe they are dangerous or just plain hopeless, keep it to yourself and don't go out with them again. Another way of making sure you are not asked out again is to be negative and moan and groan about everything. Sure the fishing may be slow, but you can be sure the skipper is acutely aware of the fact and they don't need reminding every few minutes.

Probably the best way of being labelled as a bad risk and never being asked again is to get sea sick and force the skipper to take you back to shore. Word of this happening spreads like wild fire amongst offshore fisherman and it's an act which is often remembered for years. At the time you may feel like you're dying, but if you shut your mouth and keep fishing you'll earn their respect, not their sarcasm. I'm speaking from experience with seasickness. For years I got crook every time I went out but I never asked to go back in. Sometimes with new skippers I had to argue to stay out there because I knew if I crumbled, I wouldn't be asked to go again. Eventually I stopped getting sick so if you suffer like I did, there is light at the end of the tunnel. I found that catching fish was the best way of getting over it.

Being a deckie means you have to fish for what the skipper wants to target and if he decides to move or chase something else, that's what you're doing too. This forces you to do something different to the way you prefer to fish. If you pick up the challenge rather than whinge, you'll become a better all round angler. Just about all skippers do things a little differently and the more boats you fish from the more tricks you'll pick up. Try not to preach about how good a certain style is or the 'best' way of doing things. When it comes to

A few nice Jew caught on a charter boat.

fishing, I've found the best way of getting their attention is by quietly doing my own style while making sure it doesn't interfere with their lines. If I'm obviously doing better than them then chances are they will change. If they are doing better than me, I guarantee I'll be watching like a hawk and thinking about following suit.

Try to be self-sufficient while taking up as minimal amount of space as you can. Find out before you go out what style the skipper intends to do. There is no use rigging for marlin if he is chasing snapper. If you are going to use a bait jig then tie it onto a light rod that is rigged with a quality reel carrying a good line load. This way when the bait is caught you can re-rig the rod to chase whatever you are targeting. My 'bait rod' is always pre-tied with a leader so it's quicker to turn it into a snapper or mackerel rod. Whenever possible rig your lines at home. I carry all the gear I need in a 20 litre bucket and have done for the last 30 years. This includes assorted hooks and sinkers, camera, food and drink, floats, bait, the odd lure, wire traces, knife and scaler.

A Spanish mackerel each for the deckies.

A quality wahoo caught from his mate's boat.

A nice day and a great fish for the deckie.

GAME BOATS

Game boats are a bit like yachts, they are owned by rich people who let poor people play with them. Not that I'm bagging the wealthy, without them the only way to get on a game boat would be on a charter. If you want to get on these rigs it really helps to have experience on how offshore boats work, how to fight reasonable sized fish and also gaffing or tagging them. Jumping on a game boat too early might ruin the chance of being asked to go again. Don't expect to be on the 'gun' boat of the fleet either. These skippers can afford to be picky on who gets a run on their boat.

Game boats generally troll skirted lures and the skipper is the one who decides which rod goes where and what sort of lure pattern will be run. Deckies do the work and the skipper gives the orders. Game fishing is 95% boring and 5% flat strap exciting! To fill in time and earn your passage you should be looking for birds working, plus watching that the troll lines have not tangled. Resist the temptation of sitting on a comfortable seat in the cabin because that's not fishing.

Find out the rules of the boat before you get onboard. You may have to pay your share of fuel and if it's a big boat it will be quite expensive. None of the big cruisers I went on charged for fuel. Money was not a problem for these blokes but keeping a crew of 3 or 4 keen anglers who could be relied on to front up whenever the skipper wanted to fish was harder than you may think. A lot of boats run on a system where each angler goes 'on strike' for an hour which means whoever's turn it is, they get any rod that gets a strike. Other boats give a designated rod each.

Sometimes the deckie gets lucky.

CONCLUSION

If you are going to be a deckie then do it right. Be helpful and useful without being overbearing. Remember you are the worker, not the boss. There are a lot of tips on how to be a deckie in the chapter Offshore Options so if you haven't already, give it a read. If you are asked to go fishing, don't start taking control with comments like 'If we are chasing snapper I can go.' Or 'Saturday mornings are no good because I'll have a hangover, but I could probably make it Sunday arvo.' Another classic is when asked they say, 'I'll get back to you' but they don't. The skipper is trying to do the right thing by this person, but the end result is he runs out of time to ask anyone else. People who continue to muck the skipper around invariably stop being asked. Good deckies are keen and have fishing as a priority, not an afterthought.

Venus tusk fish are great on the plate.

KIDS' FISHING

Kids' fishing is the ultimate style of family fishing. You can start them at any age and it's a great excuse to go out and sample our beautiful waterways. Safety and fun are the main requirements and if you get that right the rest will follow.

I'm constantly amazed how much kids can eat and drink during a fishing outing so pack heaps. Protection from sun and insects is essential as they have much softer skin than adults.

At 37cm this bream will probably stay his personal best for a long time.

Some will stay glued to a rod for hours while others prefer to burn energy by exploring and running around on the sand flats. Both are fine as long as you keep it safe. When kids are learning the art of fishing, the whole idea of taking them should be to put them onto fish. If you are catching more than them and they can't put the bait on or cast properly then you are doing it wrong.

At first glance there is not a lot of difference between you going fishing and taking the kids, or taking the kids fishing. Yet in practice there is a huge gap between the two. Going fishing and taking the kids, generally means you will be doing most of the fishing and they will simply be there. Taking the kids fishing means they will be fishing and you are there to advise, encourage and help them. You may even get a chance to chuck a line for yourself, but at the start, don't count on it.

Teaching youngsters to fish starts well before they get near water. Mine have grown up with rods scattered around the house and they have learnt to treat them with care. They know rods are not for playing swords or spears and when-ever they helped me carry rods out to the car, I drummed it into their heads to watch the rod tip and be careful not to jamb it into the ground, ceiling fan or in a doorway etc.

Most kids don't have the patience to sit around for hours waiting for a bite so if you want to keep them fishing it pays to target areas where the fish are smaller and more plentiful in numbers. Wharfs and jetties are ideal as are many riverbanks, especially if they have exposed sandy beaches on the run out tide.

Look for places where the current doesn't run too fast because these areas are easier to fish. Kids and fast currents don't mix. When fishing from the shore their lines constantly wash into the bank and if they are on a wharf and manage to fall in, it's much more dangerous if a fast current is present. Locations that have a clean bottom (i.e. sand or mud) are much easier to fish because of the lack of snags. When the bottom is rough and every cast is finding a snag it's no fun at all. To save your sanity you are better off moving to a place with a more forgiving bottom.

On holiday and chasing a few fish.

Kids are quite competitive and by its very nature fishing tends to teach them how to win and more importantly, how to lose. They will have days where they catch heaps and flog their mates and/or parents. Yet you can guarantee that sooner or later the boot will be on the other foot. This is the time to remind them to calm down and enjoy the fishing. Win lose or draw.

Quite often you see a kid hooked up to a good fish with their parents standing beside them; urging them on by telling them to keep winding. That's ok if you have loose line but trying to wind in when the fish is taking line is not a good angling skill and if using an eggbeater reel it produces line twist. The twist is caused by the reel's rotating bail arm. If it cannot lay line on the spool when you wind in, each rotation of the bail arm will twist the line. For those who don't know what line twist is, it's the thing that causes the annoying habit of line wrapping around the rod tip whenever there is no tension on the line. In severe cases line twist can be seen by the line twisting up on itself and tangling.To my way of thinking the biggest pain in the bum with line twist is the line wrapping around the rod tip. But from a kid's point of view the most frustrating part is getting those mysterious birds nests (tangles) in the line, often during the cast. They don't know why, but somehow the line's in a mess and chances are mum or dad is not going to be pleased. Yet it's not the kids fault and if you teach them right it will rarely become a problem.

Teaching a kid to stop winding the handle when they are not gaining line is easy if you do it right. Waiting until they are hooked up to something big is not the ideal time to be lecturing them on the principles of line twist and how to correctly play a fish. The kid's buzzing along at a million miles an hour on a huge mixture of adrenalin, excitement and fear. Often they are simply not able to concentrate on advice given from bystanders and fight the fish at the same time.

Quality time for dad and daughter.

I taught my daughter, Sandy, how to fight a fish in the back yard. I got her to cast out a small lead (definitely no hook) then close the bail arm, the same as when fishing. Then I'd grab the sinker and run around the yard like a mad boofhead, ripping line off the spool with wild arm movements. The aim of the game was for Sandy to land the fish (me) and whenever she wound while she could not gain line I would pick her up on it, likewise for keeping the rod bent. When she did it right I'd let her gain line on me, but if the rod went slack I'd take off again, just like a fish. As with all games that teach a lesson it's best to let them win because it leaves them confident and happy with their newfound fishing skills.

Things went well and Sandy quickly learned when to wind and when to just hang on. Yet so far it was all theory and I didn't know how she would react when a good fish gave her a workout. Sure she had caught her fair share of under sized models but nothing to really stretch her.

Crunch time came when I took her fishing from the bank at a local place called the Golden Hole. It's a small creek mouth coming off the main river where tidal movement is minimal and the bank is nice and flat which is perfect for kids. The first prawn to hit the water was quickly devoured by a small bream and Sandy was tickled pink with the fact she caught a fish before I even had my line in the water! It was a good start to the morning and she proceeded to flog me in the small bream stakes like only a kid can.

Calm water, perfect weather and a few fish make an awesome day.

She was feeling pretty cocky after landing about eight bream to dad's three when I cast out my light outfit and left it lying on the bank with the bail arm open. I wanted to get some action shots of Sandy catching a fish and was unpacking the camera when in a mad panic she yelled that I was loosing line. I grabbed it, closed the bail arm and gave the rod a stab and felt weight, then instantly stuck the rod in Sandy's hands. I was in photo taking mode and made a dash for the camera. As I readied the equipment I clearly remember the realization dawning on me that the weight of the fish when I sunk the hook was pretty good and maybe I'd acted a bit rash.

Meanwhile Sandy was really being stretched. The drag was set a bit tight for her to handle. It still released line every time the fish took off but you could see her working to counteract being pulled in.

The fish ran about four times and she handled it well. I was busy with the camera and didn't help her at all. Actually I was probably more of a hindrance than a help. Once when it ran away from where I was standing I told her to turn it and swim it up my way so I could get a better photo. Yep, right dad, whatever you reckon!

A quality flathead at exactly 1kg.

Finally she saw what she was fighting when a big ugly flathead slowly glided into view. The flathead was totally played out with hardly a flap left in it and

I don't think Sandy had too much left either. We didn't have a landing net but luckily it wasn't deeply hooked and we managed to slide the lizard up the bank. At 58 cm it was definitely a good flathead and being her first legal sized fish, it was one I doubt she will ever forget. Back home we put it on the lie detector and it weighed in at one kilo neat, which is a top fish for a kid.

A child needs courage to hold a fish with this mouth full of teeth

KIDS IN BOATS

I believe it's a good idea to show your kids the fundamentals of fishing from a landbased location rather than teaching them in a boat. Skipping the lessons of catching tiddlers from a wharf or sandflats doesn't help them in the long run. When they can happily fish without your help, they are ready to do it from a boat.

Boats are limited in space so when the fish are not biting kids get bored and say there is nothing to do. On the bank they can have a break and go chasing crabs or explore the other end of the beach, but in a boat they are stuck until the adult decides to move. This is a recipe for whingeing which is something any parent could do without. A good supply of munchies and drinks will stave off the moaning for a limited time frame, but expecting them to sit still for a few hours is being unrealistic.

If your area has sandflats showing on low tide then timing the trip for a falling tide can help extend your fishing time. When the kids are losing interest and rubbing you up the wrong way (and they will) instead of going home, motor over to a sandflat. They can either keep fishing or burn energy by running amok on the sand. Either way it gives everyone a bit of space and there is still a good chance of flathead and whiting.

Their safety is literally in your hands so be very careful and conservative in your actions. Most safety issues are basically common sense and if you keep an eye on them, problems can be resolved before they happen. With young kids things can go wrong incredibly quickly. I once saw a two year old girl crawl off the side of a cabin cruiser at anchor and the kid sunk like a rock. Luckily her mother was on the ball and dived overboard and got her back, but if the water had been dirty I seriously doubt the baby would have been found.

Wharves are excellent places for family fishing

When they know the basics of fishing a kid can be a real asset on a boat. They have a refreshing attitude to life and everything around them. Even when the fish aren't biting you can still pick up an insight into the way they feel about any number of issues. It seems the older they get the better they are in boats and who knows, they may become perfect deckies for doing the heavier work during our later years.

RIGS

For most situations it is best to keep the rig simple. A small ball sinker sliding directly down to a long shank 1/0 hook can be deadly effective on a wide range of species. A long shank hook helps with bait presentation if you

Whiting fight well and have no spikes which make them a perfect kid's fish.

Targeting bass is a great way to introduce kids to lure fishing.

are using prawns and it also helps if the fish takes the hook deeply. Obviously if you prefer a different hook pattern then go for it but remember that smaller gaped hooks catch more fish.

I have yet to use a swivel on a kids rig because most times they are not needed. Situations that need a heavy lead such as areas with a strong tidal flow often need a swivel to keep the lead away from the hook, but with kids these are places I tend to avoid.

Fishing the beach is a great way to entertain kids, especially if you can find a hole in close.

A common mistake made by parents is to tie on a wire trace to avoid being bitten off by flathead. The trouble is that flathead rarely bite through the line, unless it is deeply hooked and you lift their head out of the water. That's when they thrash their head from side to side, sawing through the line. If your hooks are being 'snipped' off then I would be more inclined to either blame tailor or a bad knot for the loss of your hook.

Kids have a habit of tangling fancy rigs and the less hardware that is put in the water, the better are your chances of catching fish.

RODS AND REELS

It's hard enough choosing the perfect outfit for yourself let alone finding one that is exactly right for your child. Many of us bail up on the idea of spending big dollars on a child's first rod and reel because chances are they will wreck it. The way around this is to teach them to respect their gear and not dump it on the sand when things are not going their own way.

For young kids a 6 foot rod is plenty long enough. Look for one that has a light action (bends easily) and a short butt so they don't have to stretch out to reach the reel. The rod should also be extremely light in weight because plenty of kids will put the rod down when it starts feeling heavy. This size rod is excellent for both boat and bank fishing. Carbon fibre rods should be avoided because while they are very light, they break easily.

Once they have grown up a bit, who knows what they can catch.
(Photo: Greg Hill)

There are a number of budget priced combo outfits available for kids and as with most things, you get what you pay for. What ever you do, don't fall for the trap of buying one of those $15 - $20 rod and reel combinations where the reel has a skinny spool and the bail arm is basically made of wire. There must have been millions made because they are available just about every-where. If you don't know the ones I mean, look for the cheapest, rubbishy looking units in your local fishing shop and you have found them. These things are nearly impossible for an experienced angler to cast, let alone a child.

The best style of reel for a child to learn is the one you are best able to teach them. Eggbeaters are pretty fool-proof, if you know how to use them.

When setting the drag on your child's reel it is important to remember to set it light. It's so easy to forget they are not nearly as strong as an adult and what feels right for you is often far too heavy for a young child. It's fair enough to fish heavier once they get older and know what they are doing but for youngsters, keep it light. If you have selected them a nice light action rod then it will still bend into a good working curve by the time line starts releasing from the drag and a hook-up to a just legal-sized fish should pull line from the spool and put up a good fight.

When the kid grows up they often take the parent fishing.

No chapter on kids fishing would be complete without mention of protecting them from the elements. Hats, sunscreen and insect repellent are a must and in a number of cases so are sunglasses. Apart from the bites, Ross River Fever is becoming much more wide spread and is passed on by mosquitoes which have a very wide habitat. If there is a chance of rain chuck in a rain coat for them and long pants and a jumper are handy to have if the weather turns foul.

CONCLUSION

You don't have to be a great angler to teach your child how to fish. My parents never had a clue about fishing and if it wasn't for my obsession they would never have given it a thought. The point is, every time I was taken fishing I had a great time despite the fact that none of us knew what we were doing. So don't put it off, go chuck a line with your kids. Keep your cool, keep them safe and try to put them onto fish. If you do that the rest will come naturally.

LAND BASED GAMEFISHING

For some people, the idea of catching gamefish from a land based location seems crazy. Yet, other anglers have dedicated years to the sport. There are a huge number of locations between Brisbane and Sydney, many of which will remain secret until being 'discovered' by each new generation. Getting out and exploring new territory can be good fun and extremely rewarding, even if you don't find a great spot.

From Newcastle to Sydney LBG locations are pretty well known. Virtually all of them have deep water frontage right on the edge where you stand. Unfortunately many are decorated with empty bait jig packs, old line and plastic bags, although to be fair, this attitude is changing for the better.

North of Newcastle locations tend to change. There are still the more traditional spots on the ocean end of dominant headlands but added to this are the ocean end of river breakwalls, the sea side of harbour breakwalls and a lot of sloping ledges that push into fairly shallow, sand bottomed water. At some locations the water depth changes dramatically at different times of year. I know a few spots where sand covers reef a few times per season. When the reef is showing it's a great spot for live bait but when sanded over the place is quiet.

The long walk out. The foam is lightweight comfort to keep you out there for longer. (Photo by D. Clarke)

The first time I walked out to the point at Hat Head I was very disappointed. The water looked fairly shallow and it didn't seem like you would get much of a drift. There was no real comfy place to camp beside your rod while waiting for a strike and most of the 'platform' sloped down and out into the water making it difficult collecting water to store live baits. I didn't think I was in the right place but I was. Basically it was a case of 'welcome to the North Coast'. The flat sandstone ledges down towards Sydney are replaced by un-even, rough volcanic rock. That same day I watched another newcomer skating over the rocks because he was wearing cleats (steel studs) in his shoes as a safety measure. These things are said to work well on sandstone but on hard volcanic rock, cleats are deadly.

While it seems I've given Hat Head a bad rap, most of the North Coast ledges are very similar. On the plus side Hat Head is a top spot for northern bluefin tuna and is pretty good for cobia, mackerel, kings and even the odd small black marlin. It takes a bit of practice to change your perception of a classic LBG location but once you do, the North Coast and Southern Queensland have a lot going for them.

BAITS

Live baits are best and a plastic blow-up kid's pool is used to keep them alive. To fill it you'll need a bucket on a rope which is dropped into the ocean and pulled out with the rope. The bucket needs to be solid and if it's too big it will be really hard to lift when full. A battery operated aerator (or two) is used to keep the bait in good condition and a fresh bucket of water poured in every now and again also helps, especially if the day is hot.

An excellent kingfish and the gear used to catch it.
(Photo by S. Santoro)

The most common baitfish caught is yellowtail, commonly called yakkas, and they are also the hardiest and are good baits. My all time favourite bait is big slimy mackerel but you don't get them nearly enough and without proper care they are the first to die. Pike and garfish are also good.

Normally the water is burleyed with a mix of well mashed wet bread with the odd munched pilchard for taste. The trick with burley is to use a little bit often. Hopefully bait fish will react to the burley and can be caught with a bait jig. If that doesn't work the bait jig can be cast out wide and jigged back.

A quality bluefin with the 'Slider rig' used to catch it. (Photo by S. Santoro)

At some locations bait is almost guaranteed but at others more often than not there will be no baitfish available. This is when lures or pilchards come into play. Live tailor are often the first choice for Spanish mackerel specialists and are generally sent straight back out wearing a few hooks and a wire trace. Big tailor don't live too long in the pools but 2 possibly 3 just legal ones survive fairly well. Further south salmon are often overlooked as a baitfish but kings and big tuna will take them.

Once you get your bait in the water, the hope is to get a good drift so it pushes out wide. Drifts are water currents that head out and are similar to a rip on the beach. They are either fuelled by ocean currents or a back surge from a wave that has broken on the rocks. Even without a good drift, with patience and a bit of skill you can 'swim' your bait out a fair way. Baits don't always have to be out wide to get hit. If you can park one just on the outside edge where the white water is boiling out, it's in a prime spot. This is a great spot to park a 'slider' as well.

When the bait is in a comfortable spot with a constantly taut line, most anglers stand their rod in a tight fitting crevice with the ratchet on with the drag set light, but making really sure the drag is heavy enough to stop an over-run. A safety line clipped to the reel and the other end tied to a solid lump of rock is good insurance because when you get a hit they roar off fast. This safety line is generally the same rope used on the bucket to get water and has a dog clip tied to one end. Some anglers prefer to lay the rod down flat with a big rock on the rod butt to hold it in place, using a safety line as well. The problem with this style is you need a good drop-off in front of the rod to clear the line from barnacles etc.

I know a few blokes who don't bother chasing live bait. They fish a pilchard on gang hooks under a float using their spin gear and have caught bluefin, spotted mackerel, bonito and Mac tuna as well. They also score tailor and these are sent out on the big gear.

Occasionally these blokes get energetic and put in some time casting surface poppers, stick baits or metal slugs. Yet they have their 'lazy' style down pat and prefer to lay back, take it easy and spin yarns instead of lures.

One time 4 or 5 of us had livies under floats drifting out wide. A few yellowfin had been hooked in the previous days and we were all keen to get one ourselves. The sea was flat and crystal clear. We had burleyed a large school of yakkas that had been hanging around for hours when two big kings slowly cruised into view.

What surprised me was the way the baitfish acted. They stayed calm and the school parted like the kings were encased in an invisible bubble. The kings cruised right through the middle of the school without touching them and kept on patrolling along the rock face. We were all amazed and one bloke wound his line in close hoping it would get

High ledges generally mean deep water in close. Kings like these conditions. (Photo by D. Clarke)

hit. It must have been in their line of sight but was left untouched. Not long after the kings came back and still showed no interest in the school of bait. The bloke with his line in close decided to change his live bait.

As soon as the panicking and vibrating fresh bait hit the water, one of the kings peeled off at speed and monstered it. The king did what most of them do, roared along the rock face quickly rubbing through the line. This was one of those lessons I'll never forget. You don't have to be out wide to catch fish and a fresh, panicking bait is far superior to one that is 'comfortable' with its surroundings.

RIGS

Hook size is dictated by the bait being used. Garfish are great bait but they don't handle big hooks. A single light to medium gauge 5/0 pinned down towards the tail is a good rig for garfish.

For yellowtail and slimy mackerel a 6/0 to 8/0 is fine. Big tailor can easily handle one or two 10/0's. The line class being used also has a bearing on hook selection. There is no sense using heavy duty 10/0's if you are fishing 6kg line, or thin gauge hooks with 24kg line.

I like a 3 or 4 metre wind-on leader of roughly twice the breaking strain of the main line. A lot of anglers go for a much heavier leader but I think that only cuts down on the amount of strikes you get. But, if you like a heavier leader, go for it. If it is mackerel season and you are north of Port Macquarie then it is recommended to run a wire trace. Check the mackerel chapter for the best rigs. Some people claim bluefin are a wire shy fish but I've caught enough to know they don't seem to mind a short single strand trace. Torpedo floats are most commonly used and the knot of the wind-on leader doubles as the stopper knot for the float. The maximum depth of your bait is dictated by the length of the leader.

A trophy sized Spanish mackerel off the stones.

Rod lengths vary between angler preferences. Some like shorter rods but if you are fishing the North Coast or Southern Queensland, a 10 or even 12 foot rod won't be out of place. If getting the rod custom built, go for fairly wide runners so the leader knot runs through the guides easier. Rockfishing is hard on gear so go for runners that are not too lightweight.

GAFFING

When you finally hook-up and work the fish in close, it's generally a team effort to land it. While you can sometimes wash a fish up a series of ledges with the waves, it's a lot more common for someone to gaff it. This can be an extremely dangerous time because with all the excitement and pressure of a big fish, it's not too hard to forget to watch the waves. If you are the person on the gaff you have to hold your safety as the number one priority. Don't be ordered onto an obviously dangerous spot by an over-anxious angler. In the heat of the moment, his mind could be totally concerned with the fish, not you.

With teeth like these you need a wire trace.

Due to the locations being fished, gaffs need to be long and at many places a gaff shorter than 3 metres is almost a waste of time carrying it out there. They can be awkward things to handle and most people don't get to use them very often. The best way I can describe using them is to hold the gaff so the hook point is facing away from the rocks. This helps hold the hook in while lifting and dragging the fish out. If you gaff them with the point facing the rocks there is a fair chance of the fish rolling off the gaff as you lift and drag it up the rock-face. When you get a shot at the fish it is with a sharp solid lift, preferably into the front end of the fish in the stomach or chest area. This keeps the fish pointing towards you so any thrashing of its tail helps you lift it. Ideally you should come in with the gaff shot behind the line so if you miss, the fishing line doesn't get tangled or wrapped around the gaff. Because the gaff is so long, you have to make a conscious effort to watch both ends of the gaff so the line will clear it, while still keeping an eye on incoming waves. Nothing is easy about land based gamefishing. If you muck up a gaff shot it will haunt you for weeks. Yet if you kill yourself trying, it will haunt everyone else for the rest of their lives.

A big hook-up on a quiet section of rocks.

When I was a young bloke, life jackets were big cumbersome things that were really hot when you had them on, so no-one wore them. Occasionally I saw rock fisherman in wetsuits but they gave the same problem of overheating you as well. Now-days they are called PFD's (personal flotation devices) and they are much more user friendly. Certain councils in Sydney have made the use of PFD's compulsory while rockfishing in their shire because of the amount of deaths from drowning. I can see this being extended all up and down the coast. These days by law I have to wear one in my boat and on the kayak and honestly, I forget I'm wearing it because they are so lightweight and unobtrusive.

PUTTING IN THE TIME

It's great when you get there and everything works. Bait is easy to catch and soon you have a screaming reel. Yet for every one of those days you will have 10 or more very quiet ones. Nothing beats putting in the hours during the right time of year so it is helpful to extend your time on the rocks while you are there. If you arrive at daylight and leave at 10am you will have fished through prime time and put in a good effort. Although if you stay until 1pm then your chances of hooking a fish are better, even though the last few hours could be considered as a quiet time for fishing. I've seen some pretty big fish caught in the middle of the day so it is not a waste of time.

A few days of southerly wind tends to push the warm water currents in closer to shore. So if the swell is not big or you know a sheltered location tucked in on the northern side of a headland, it's a good time to be on the rocks.

A quality kingfish caught in the middle of a city.
(Photo by S. Santoro)

Taking enough food and drink is one of the easiest ways of extending your fishing time. Another way is to stay active. Once you are comfortable with where your bait is sitting and you have your rod set, you can try for something else. It may be more bait, bream or a spot of casting with lures or plastics for whatever is hungry. Don't go too far from your main rod, because after all, that's the one you want to go off and it has first priority.

Times when you have previously been burleying for an hour or two chasing bait are excellent for a change to bream. You just swap the bait jig for a 1/0 hook and a tiny sinker and fish a bait in close to the rocks. Drummer is another great option after burleying but you'll need heavier line to land them.

LBG takes a lot of dedication and time to be successful. You also need to be reasonably fit because a fair amount of gear needs to be carried and many of the locations are quite a hike from the car park. Being an organized person certainly helps because there is a lot of preparation to be done before you leave home. Forgetting things like spare bait jigs, the gaff or the pool to put your bait in can ruin the day, or at least make it a lot harder.

CONCLUSION

LBG is not for everyone, far from it. The reels need to be high quality and able to hold a huge amount of line and many of the rods used are custom built. Hook-ups are few and far between and when you finally do bang the hook into a good one, it's even harder to land it. If you are the type of angler who has to catch fish every time you chuck a line for the outing to be successful, then this style will drive you crazy.

Dedication, persistence and a sense of achievement simply by going through the motions certainly helps. I know I still get a warm glow when I cast out a live bait using a big lever drag reel and get a reasonable distance without mucking it up by fuzzing the reel. This style pushes you to become fanatical about your gear, your knots and your whole way of fishing. It also gives you plenty of time to think about it.

Simply enjoying being there is a big bonus in your favour. The true LBG experience is as much about the journey as it is about finally landing a monster, then struggling to carry it back to the car.

MACKEREL

Two types of mackerel migrate down the NSW North Coast, Spanish mackerel and spotted mackerel. Heading north they can be found right around the Top End and a fair way down the WA Coast.

Port Macquarie is recognised as the southern point of the mackerel's migration. Some years they don't reach Port while occasionally they run a lot further south. It all depends on the currents. Yet every year they reach Crescent Head, the first town north of Port Macquarie.

At South West Rocks spotted mackerel are the first to arrive, generally in late December and are a welcome addition to the Christmas school holidays.

This first run are generally smaller fish around 3kg but what they lack in size is more than made up for with a frenzied style of feeding. This red hot bite only lasts for a week or so and if weather conditions are good, a lot of fish are caught.

Their larger cousins, the Spanish, turn up in numbers a few weeks later. Again at South West Rocks, the season ends roughly mid June. The further north you travel, the longer the season becomes.

They prefer water temps of 21C and above. When the water is deep blue and 25 or more degrees, you are fishing in prime time.

A little spottie caught on a trolled pilchard. Note the rod rigger used to keep a good spread while trolling.

Mackerel can be found anywhere from 100 metres water depth to virtually the shore. Yet the vast majority of mackerel are targeted on reefs within one to three kilometres from the shore. I suspect the close reefs are where they hold up for a while, ambushing baitfish around the pinnacles. Fish caught out wide are probably travellers running with the currents. Many of the most productive mackerel reefs are straight out from large dominant headlands.

The things to look for when working the sounder are bait schools and pinnacles or high points in the reef. Ideally the sounder screen will show tight balls of bait with markings of bigger fish around the outside. Yet more often than not, if you can find a good set of pinnacles with plenty of bait in the water your chances of action are quite good. Mackerel are also attracted to islands, especially if they are part of a larger reef system. While reef areas are a good place to start, don't forget to watch for bait schools. We've had some magic days fishing among bait schools over a sand bottom.

When the ocean is 'glassing out' spotted mackerel often come on the bite.

Southerly winds tend to push in warm currents close to shore and fishing can be quite good once the seas calm down after a southerly blow. Dirty water from floods often tends to push mackerel out wider in search of clean water. Most anglers simply chase snapper until the water clears but if you're keen and go wide and find a demarcation line between clean and dirty water the fishing can be hot.

Late in the season mackerel have a habit of leaving the close reefs and moving out to depths of 40 to 50 metres. Some years they stay out there for a week or so then move back in close, other times they are on the bite out wide one day then in close the next, then back out wide a day or so later.

Mackerel have a habit of being extremely frustrating for many anglers.

From first light until 9am is the most productive time so you need to be on the water early. They can still be caught after 9am but most days the bite does tend to taper off. More importantly, bait fish are also a lot easier to catch before the sun is too high. Late afternoon is also productive but strong north easterly winds are common after mid-day and make planning a trip difficult. North easterlies are the worst wind for smallish boats because it makes the sea extremely sloppy quite quickly.

This monster mackerel went 38kg. (Photo by L. Williams)

Mackerel are a big powerful fish and the use of a gaff is essential. The best place to gaff them is in the gills or chest area. This gives a solid purchase point and brings them into the boat head first. You could be really professional and hook them through the bottom jaw so no flesh is spoilt, but the truth is any gaff shot that lands the fish is a good one. The idea is to come in from behind the line and underneath the fish. This way if you miss, the fish will blast off without the line wrapped around the gaff handle and if you get it, the shaft of the gaff guides the hook in and there is less chance of the fish rolling off the hook. A proper gaff shot is done with a sharp straight lift not swung like a club.

LIVE BAIT

Targeting mackerel with live bait is the most popular and productive style in southern areas. Slimy mackerel and pike are my favourites and yellowtail are pretty good on them as well. If the area you are fishing has legal sized tailor then use them as they are excellent on Spanish.

Strangely enough, some of the best days we have had are when baits are very hard to catch. Plenty of anglers forget the mackerel and chase snapper when livies are hard to find. This sort of thinking is fair enough when targeting a feed but there is always a chance you are passing on some top fishing. Being patient and putting in the extra effort to catch quality bait is often the difference between success and failure.

Pike are a great bait for spanish.

During the mackerel season local bait grounds are not hard to find. Just look for a cluster of boats with anglers using bait jigs or ask some of the locals. Most bait grounds are close to the launch site and anglers load up their bait tanks before the short trip to the mackerel reef. Sometimes you can go straight to where you intend to fish and catch the bait on site. This is especially relevant to pike as the first reef is often where they are the thickest.

Very early in the morning is the best time for pike and there is a bit of a trick to catching them. They like a rough peaky bottom, with a fair amount of weed growth. The most effective rig is a reasonably small ball sinker running directly onto a 1/0 long shank hook with a smallish strip of mullet for bait. The hook is passed once only, through one end of the strip of bait, leaving a free flowing tail to entice them. The majority of pike are caught between half a metre to three metres off the bottom and a moving bait has a far better chance of being taken than one anchored to the bottom. Plenty of strikes occur when feeding the bait down through the strike zone and if you don't get a hit on the way down, wind up 5 or 10 turns and repeat the process.

When using a single hook it is best to give them two or three seconds to get the bait in their mouth before striking. Some anglers use two 1/0 hooks linked together claiming this rig is better for catching them, but the extra hook is a lot harder to get out and often badly damages the pike. They will also take a pilchard but again, the gang hooks do damage them.

Pike have a good set of teeth and they can bite through your line so to get around the problem we use a 15kg leader. Even with the leader there is often

the need to re-tie the hook due to line damage. Pike are not nearly as good as tailor when it comes to biting people, but they do have a good set of choppers that need to be treated with respect. I've never been bitten by one, but then again, I don't want to either.

If your boat does not have a bait tank then a large plastic rubbish bin or a big esky will do at a pinch, as long as the water stays fresh by regular changes. Ideally a live bait tank should have clean circulating water pumped through via a bilge pump. Big live baits (the best kind for Spanish) need to be looked after to be effective because they lose a lot of their appeal when they are half dead.

This fish took a snapper bait and emptied the line load right down to the knot.

Pike, large slimy mackerel, tailor and bonito are the best baits for Spanish mackerel. Spotted mackerel prefer a more modest bait such as small to average sized slimy mackerel. As with most things to do with fishing there is a fair overlap in the 'rules' and it is possible to catch spotted mackerel on large pike and Spanish on small slimies.

FLOATS

Baits are set roughly 2 or 3 metres under the float, although if diving birds are a problem it pays to set them deeper. A good idea is to stagger the depths when a number of live baits are fished from the one boat. That way more water is covered and it is sometimes possible to predict what depth they are feeding on the day. Very deeply set baits, say 15 metres, will often find their own depth and cannot be expected to be found straight under the float.

While anchored, live baits are hooked up facing away from the float so there is less chance of the line fouling on the wire trace or hooks. The exception is when the current is boiling through because at these times they can be safe-ly fished nose into the current without a float. Unexplained bite offs can often be the result of loose line between the float and the bait catching on the hooks and being sliced when the bait is attacked. Deeply set baits are more prone to this problem.

A popular float is a cube of styrofoam with a knife slice all the way around it. The line is half hitched twice into the knife slice at the required depth. If the line doesn't go into the knife slice there is a chance the line will break when you get a strike. When a mackerel hits a bait the foam 'pops', leaving you in direct contact with the fish. To date the pollution aspect of using a float that only lasts one strike has yet to be addressed, but it does seem to be a most successful arrangement.

Wet weather doesn't slow down keen fishermen when spotted mackerel are about.

Torpedo floats can also be used but there is always the chance of them being attacked by other mackerel when they are dragged behind a hooked fish. To set the depth with a torpedo float I either use the knot of the leader line or the knot of a 'double' tied in the main line. Either way the depth of the bait is determined by the length of the leader or the doubled main line.

FIGHTING STYLE

It is very rare that mackerel run the line on reef and when it does its more luck than good management by the fish. A mackerel's main weapon is its awesome speed and ability to quickly cover a large distance. One of their tricks is to run directly at you, giving them a chance to spit or shake the hooks free due to no tension on the line. Their teeth are pretty mean as well and loose line in front of their mouth can result in a snip off. When it feels like you have dropped the fish it is wise to wind in as fast as possible because they might be running at you. There's no future in trying to stop them running because the hooks will pull or the line will bust. Mackerel don't have an abundance of stamina and they burn out reasonably fast but if you push the point too early you are virtually guaranteed to lose them. Once they get over 16 kilo they have quite a bit of staying power and become a totally different proposition. As you never really know how big the fish is that you have hooked, it's best to be conservative and take your time.

A lot of mackerel scream off on a good run but occasionally you will find fish that refuse to run too far. These can be a real handful near the boat and they are often the ones that give anglers the most problems. Because they are still fresh and powerful, directing them is difficult and they often go for the anchor rope.

If one does wrap your line around the anchor rope the best way to get them free is to back the drag off and keep slight tension on the spool with your thumb. Figure out which direction the line is wrapped (clock wise or anti-clock wise) then thread the rod and reel around the rope until the line is free. The first few times it happens really gets the stress levels high but after a while it's more of an embarrassment to your ego for allowing them to get there in the first place. Mates and I had plenty of practice at unwrapping them when we first started targeting them but these days we've got our act together and it doesn't happen too often. We have yet to lose any of these speedsters due to fouling the anchor rope so it's not the end of the world when it happens. It should be noted that this happened in open boats with easy access to the anchor rope. It is not nearly as easy in a lot of half cabins.

MOORING PATTERNS

Because of the mackerel's running ability boats need to be moored a fair way apart. Anchored boats generally line up along or across the reef in a loose zigzag pattern so their baits are able to float out the back of the boat into clean water without the worry of someone else's anchor rope.

When looking for a decent place to join the line, always travel on the anchor rope side of the moored boats and constantly scan the water ahead for

floats. Moored boats generally nose into the current which sends the baits out the back, but on windy days or those without current, someone's bait could be swimming anywhere.

After going to the trouble of catching quality bait and finding a good position, there is

The teeth of a Spanish mackerel deserve respect and a wire trace.

nothing more frustrating than someone invading your space by anchoring or trolling too close. Often it is a lack of experience or the anglers are too keen to get in on the action. Sometimes it's pure ignorance. Yet when the word's out about a hot mackerel bite the close reefs are becoming more crowded each year.

Much of the angler etiquette involved is common sense. Drifting or trolling through a mob of anchored boats is not the right thing to do, nor is muscling in on a boat that's catching fish. The use of light line at the more popular locations is not a great idea either. Mackerel on light gear can cover a lot of water before being subdued and there is a big chance of fouling the line on another boat's anchor rope.

LURES

One of the great things about trolling lures is it is clean, instant fishing. The moment you drop a lure out the back you are in with a chance. If you or your crew are prone to sea sickness then keeping on the move is a great way of getting a few more hours on the water, or even being out there in the first place.

Landing a good Spanish is the best way to relieve stress.

Spanish like a large lure while spotties will take almost anything when they are keen. Large deep divers take a lot of pressure to drag them at speed and a heavy line class is needed. Trolling speed with lures is generally quite fast and ranges between 8 and 15 knots. Always use the ratchet when trolling.

Rod riggers are great for widening your spread. They are designed to sit in your existing rod holders and hold the rod straight out 90 degrees to the boat and level with the water. Good ones come with safety clips that connect to your reel. Outfits used in rod riggers cop a lot of water during a session and if your reel cannot handle saltwater when the drag is set on strike, then it's no good for this sort of work.

A sneaky way of finding out what lures are working in your area is to check out what other anglers are using when they are getting ready to launch or coming back in after fishing, as most people will have their rods rigged. You can learn a lot from having a quick yarn with someone who has just had a successful session. Local tackle shops are also worth a shot and if you catch one on one of their lures, go back and tell them to keep the gossip chain moving.

Some anglers run the larger lures without wire, claiming the lure's action in the water is better without it and they are never completely inhaled. I prefer a homemade single strand trace of about 80lb with a good quality snap on the end. It is easy to change lures and I don't believe the lure's action is impeded. The trace is not because of fear the lure will be swallowed, but rather to protect your line from scrubbing against their teeth during the many direction changes during the fight.

At 9.5kg this is a perfect eating size Spanish.

The further south mackerel travel, the fussier they become, to the point where they are far from easy to catch on lures. Yet it can be done even though most anglers go for the easier option of live baiting. When fishing at anchor there are still opportunities for lures. Those occasional days where mackerel are cruising along the burley trail right to the back of the boat are ideal for casting metal pilchard imitations, soft plastics or even stick baits.

Whatever lures you try, make sure the trebles, hook connections and tow points are strong enough for the job because mackerel have a habit of finding weak points.

SPANISH MACKEREL

The average sized Spanish ranges between 8kg and 15kg although fish well over 20 kg are caught every year and occasionally big brutes over 30 kilo are landed. Spanish mackerel have been recorded to grow to 70 kilo. All the big ones are females as males rarely grow to more than 17 kilo in weight.

These fish are extremely fast and for many anglers, mackerel are the fastest fish they will ever encounter. Big Spaniards can lower your reel's line load at an incredible pace, especially if they get it into their head to run for the horizon. I like it when they go for broke and do a big distance on their opening run. It's exciting as hell and they are generally burnt out enough to not play up too much at the side of the boat.

Solid head shakes during the fight are an excellent sign you have hooked a Spanish. Sharks mauling your fish often feel like head shakes, but the difference is that after your fish has been 'sharked' it turns into a dead weight that doesn't run any more.

30 odd years ago when I first started chasing mackerel I was a big fish fanatic. I had a serious case of tunnel vision and over-sized Spanish were my target. I quickly got to the stage where I wouldn't even photograph any smaller than 14kg because it simply wasn't big enough. For years I reckoned that spotted mackerel were only a 'consolation prize', something that ripped off quality baits destined for something bigger. Boy has my attitude changed.

I'd drifted away from competition fishing around the same time that Spanish were very thin in the water, but spotties were around in good numbers. To keep that big fish feeling I dropped down in line class and found they were really top fun! I reckon I'll always think Spanish are the trophy fish but now when I join the 'Mackerel Club' it's a good day when I put any mackerel in the boat.

In NSW there has been a few cases of ciguatera poisoning and authorities have stopped pro fisherman from sending Spanish mackerel over 10kg to the markets. Very few people get this poisoning, I know of two cases in our area. Both fish were over 20kg and they were a few years back. Since then I know of heaps of big Spanish being caught and eaten with no problems. The trouble is it could happen and the idea of poisoning my family doesn't sit real well. I for one will be releasing any monster mackerel I catch.

LINE CLASS

Because Spaniards are clean water fighters they can be safely targeted with reasonably light line. 6 kilo is as light as I've been game enough to try. Average sized Spanish are not too much of a problem on 6 kilo if you take it very easy and have a lot of time and space on your side. Yet once they stack on a bit of weight, light line makes it extremely difficult to direct them and occasionally near the end of the fight they circle the boat with tenacity more becoming of bluefin tuna. These are often fish that didn't run for the horizon and saved their stamina for close to the boat, or they are simply big.

Line between 8 and 15 kilo is most commonly used and the reel needs a good capacity to be effective. 400 metres is probably enough for 10 kg, but unless you chase them with the boat it will not always be enough for 8 kg line.

My favourite line class is 8 kilo because it is light enough for the fish to put on a good show, yet strong enough to gently direct the fish when it comes close to the boat. Being able to direct them with sideways pressure when they are cruising towards the anchor rope has obvious benefits.

It's great when you can catch big fish like this within 500 metres of the ramp.

I know a few people who are still monster mackerel fanatics and they run 24 kg lines.

RIGS

Mackerel have a mouth full of extremely sharp teeth and the use of a wire trace is essential. Single strand has the advantage of being stronger when compared to the same thickness in multi-strand. This means that single strand traces are less conspicuous when using the same breaking strain which is why I prefer it. Single strand is also harder for mackerel to chew threw. On the down side single strand is easier to kink which weakens it considerably. Never send out a bait when the trace is kinked because it will probably break at the worst possible moment.

Many anglers use 60 to 100 pound traces on Spanish mackerel and 40 pound traces for spotted mackerel. Yet for a lot of years mates and I used 38 pound single strand on both species and rarely lost a fish due to wire failure. These days on 2 hook rigs I run 60 to 80lb wire between the hooks and 38lb single wire for Spanish or 27lb single wire for Spotties. It should be noted that 8kg is the heaviest line I use on mackerel. If you are running heavier line then you would need heavier trace wire to suit.

Caught on a pike, this Spanish took a huge amount of line before it was landed. (Photo: S. Johns)

The life span of these lighter traces is not very long as the wire tends to coil up after fighting a fish and occasionally the wire needs replacing after its first battle. If the fish is deeply hooked or there is any doubt about the trace, it's better to leave the hooks in the fish and tie on a new rig. Long nosed pliers are essential equipment to get hooks out of a mackerel's mouth and sometimes even they are not long enough to use safely.

Most anglers make their own wire traces, complete with black swivels and the required amount of hooks. These are stored singly, coiled in snap-lock plastic bags. Some are rigged with two hooks and some with three hooks. This gives a good coverage on different sized live baits. Hooks are pinned lightly along the back line of the fish, above the lateral line. Anglers new to the game generally shy off the idea of so many hooks but mackerel are masters at ripping off baits without finding the hooks. The hooks are linked to each other via a swivel. This stretches the hook points out a bit and gives the bait a lot more freedom of movement.

The necessary trace length is roughly half a metre long which is what we use, although some anglers go for traces of up to two metres. I believe long traces are too bulky and tend to make the fish shy away from the bait. Long heavy traces are good on sharks but not great for mackerel.

The most basic rig is a single 6/0 to 8/0 hook on half a metre of wire. This rig will catch mackerel although a large amount of strikes will be missed. More hooks are needed to increase the hook-up rate and they are either joined together with a swivel, or a 'stinger' hook is joined to the system on a short length of wire.

SPANISH MACKEREL LIVE BAIT RIG

A few years back this was the most common rig used while live baiting for Spanish. These days many manufactures are making the barbs on a lot of hooks much smaller, which makes the size swivel you use a lot more critical. Yet they still catch a lot of fish so I have kept them in.

At first glance it's easy to think there are too many hooks and hardware for a bait fish to carry. Yet this is an effective rig as mackerel are masters at getting bait off the hooks. Large baits do not have a problem carrying the weight as long as they are lightly pinned along the back. The swivels help spread the hooks and also allow the bait fish freedom of movement.

1. The required number of hooks are linked together by swivels. This is done by opening the eye of the hook and feeding the swivel around the shaft of the hook. Be careful that the swivel cannot pass over the barb of the hook, otherwise the rig is useless because it falls apart.

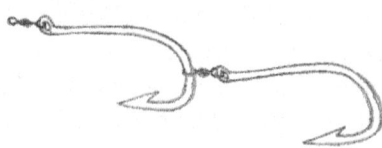

2. Once the hooks are linked they are joined to roughly half a metre of single strand wire. 38 or 44 pound wire is a popular choice. The correct tie for single strand is a haywire twist followed by a barrel roll.

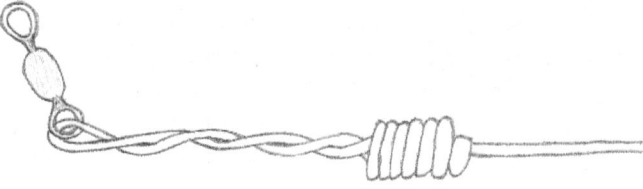

3. The finished product. When targeting mackerel it pays to pre-rig a number of traces with varying numbers of hooks and store them separately in snap lock sandwich bags.

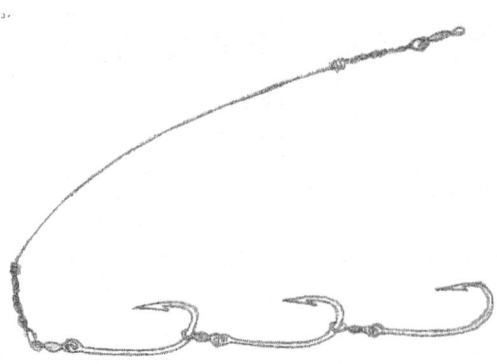

LIVEBAIT TROLLING

Trolling livebait is a style that has gained a lot in popularity. Troll speed is very slow and old 2 stroke motors tended to oil up when idled for hours. Four stroke motors don't suffer this problem.

Trace style for trolling is almost the same as those used at anchor. When trolling I like a slightly longer trace with a bit more distance between the two hooks. I prefer a two hook stinger rig when trolling because the bait has a lot more freedom of movement and is less prone to spinning.

Trolling more than three baits is begging for tangles, especially on the turns. A staggered trolling pattern helps to minimise tangled lines. Rod riggers help to spread the baits but if the current is running hard, wind is blowing or a big swell is rolling in, it is best to cut back to 2 baits. Actually, 2 baits are a lot easier to handle than 3.

Trolling is an excellent way of finding fish on quiet days where the more traditional grounds are not performing. Sometimes it's a case of finding bait schools to find the mackerel. Often they hold on the edge of a reef on the down current side because this is where bait tends to congregate. For best results troll over reef and give anglers fishing at anchor a wide berth. Downriggers have proven their worth, especially on quiet days when the mackerel are holding deep.

Knowing your area will allow you to mark on the GPS peaks and patches of reef with a history of producing fish so you can troll from one hot spot to the next.

If bonito or other small breeds of tuna are available it pays to try and catch some because they make excellent live bait for trolling. They don't survive in the bait tank as they are often too large so you need a rod rigged and ready for when one is caught. Big Spaniards will hit any tuna under about 2 kilo so don't be worried about the bait being too big. When hooking up tuna for live bait it is best to hold the fish upside down because they don't play up as much.

We use a two hook stinger rig as shown in the diagram. Live tuna are deadly on Spaniards and mates and I have found catching the tuna is often the hardest part of the deal. Once you have a tuna swimming out the back it's generally only a matter of time before its monstered. When using bonito or tuna as bait, run it on the rod with the heaviest line because chances are something really big will hit it.

TROLL RIG FOR LIVE TUNA

This rig is ideal for trolling live tuna when targeting trophy sized Spanish mackerel.

The lead hook takes the weight and is either hooked through the top jaw or horizontally through the nose. The stinger hook is lightly pinned down near the tail making sure the wire is not tight and there is plenty of hook point showing. Tuna to roughly 1 kilo are an ideal size and can be caught on casted metal lures or by trolling Christmas tree or squid style lures. Once you have the bait rigged up and swimming, troll speed is reasonably slow.

A smaller, lighter version designed to fit slimy mackerel or pike is good for trolling and also when fishing at anchor. This is the rig I currently use.

The haywire twist and barrel roll is the 'knot' to use with single strand and the arrows show directions to break off flush.

1. Take an almost metre length of 80 to 100 pound single strand wire and tie a solid swivel to one end and a 9/0 or 10/0 hook on the other end. This is the lead hook and its eye must be completely closed or the wire may catch in the gap and either fall out or cause a weak spot.

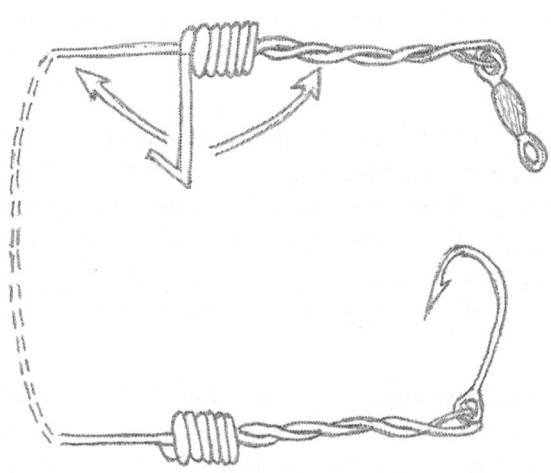

2. Take another length of the same poundage wire roughly 40cm and tie it to the eye of the hook used in step one. Tie another 9/0 hook onto the end of the shorter wire. This is the stinger hook.

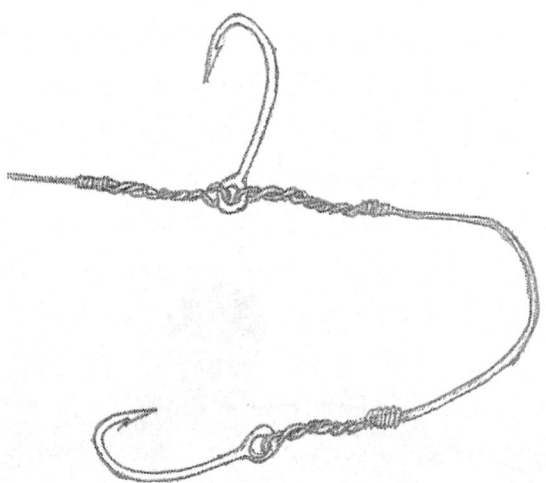

3. The finished product, a tuna rigged for trolling.

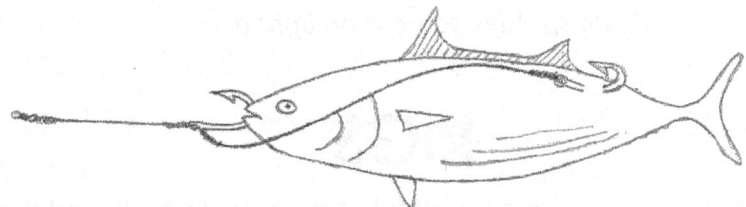

SPOTTED MACKEREL

Spotted mackerel grow to around 10 kilo, although fish of this size are rare. To date my best is 8 kilo and an average one is 4 kilo. They are a schooling fish, yet the really big ones tend to be loners. Spotties are easier to catch than Spanish as there seems to be a lot more of them in the water.

Big spotties go hard on light gear.

RIGS

These fish are equipped with a mouthful of really sharp teeth and the use of a wire trace is essential. You could get away with shop bought wire traces but I prefer to make my own with 27 pound single strand wire. Some anglers use multi strand traces but I steer clear of them because for its breaking strain it's far too thick and bulky for my liking.

There are two types of traces I use for them. The first is simplicity itself, starting with a black swivel then 30 to 40cm of 27lb single strand wire tied to a 2/0 to 5/0 hook. The wire connection on the swivel and hook is a haywire twist and barrel roll. This rig is designed for floating down strip baits.

The second rig is exactly the same as the first with a 'stinger' hook added. The stinger is another hook tied on a short length of 60-80 lb wire then tied to the eye of the first hook. I design these so the first hook goes through the eye of a pilchard and the stinger hook fits in nicely down near the tail. This rig is extremely effective on both pilchards and live baits. The reason for the heavy wire between the hooks is because that is the area that gets most of the wear from the mackerel's teeth.

For the last few seasons on some, but not all, of my traces I've been adding a ball sinker directly onto the wire between the line and the bait. With a variety of lead sizes I can cover the whole water column while drifting using pilchards. On a number of occasions I've come back to the ramp with a really good catch and no one else has got any. I'd found them feeding near the bottom while the other anglers were only fishing the top. These are also good rigs when drifting with wind, or when mutton birds are attacking 'floating' baits. You can run lead on your fishing line but it does tend to tangle the fishing line around the swivel and wire trace.

STRIP BAITS

Early in the season spotted mackerel are generally an excellent proposition for a well presented strip bait, especially when burley is used. The fresher the bait the better and the best presentation is by pushing the single hook once through an end of the bait strip. This gives a really neat presentation that doesn't spin with the current and has an excellent hook-up rate as long as the strips are not too long and there is plenty of hook point showing. Do not try to thread the bait onto the hook as you will end up with a bunched up, bruised lump of flesh and skin that will spin in the current and have a far lower hook-up rate. Single hooks work on halved pilchards as well.

Strip baits are cast out and allowed to waft down to the bottom. If for example you are anchored in 15 meters water depth with very little current, you will have to keep the casts short, otherwise you will probably snag the bottom. The opposite applies to deeper water and/or stronger current, although you don't have to run baits out wide for spotties because they are not scared of the boat. Mullet strips or the filleted side of a fresh slimy mackerel make the best strip baits.

PILCHARDS AND LIVE BAITS

As mentioned earlier, I use the same two hook rig for pilchards and live baits.

The pilchard is rigged with the head facing the angler as it tends to spin less and it is fished the same way as strip bait. I prefer the two hooks rather than a set of gang hooks because it is much lighter and doesn't sink as fast, plus it also presents the bait better and has a better hook-up rate.

Unlike pilchards, live baits are rigged with the fishes head pointing away from the angler. The lead hook is put in down near the tail above the lateral line, and the stinger hook is lightly pinned high in their back up near their head. The hook near the tail carries the weight while the stinger just goes along the ride. Having the bait constantly swimming away from you keeps the line tight and there is less chance of the bait swimming back around and tangling around your line. This is the reason for a lot of unexplained bite offs. The only time I'll fish live baits facing towards me is when anchored and the current is running strong or while drifting fairly fast due to wind. Under these conditions a float is not necessary.

Early season spotties are not big but they are keen to feed.

Generally live baits need to be fished under a float, otherwise they will seek shelter in the reef and that is where your hooks will stay. I set the bait approximately 2 or 3 meters from the float as spotted mackerel are surface feeders, yet when things are quiet or diving birds are a problem I'll run one down deep to see if that's where the action is.

Small to medium sized slimy mackerel are the ultimate live bait, followed by yellowtail. If the only live baits you can catch are big then don't be too worried because they still work. The down side to big live baits is spotties often slash them to bits without actually hooking up. Yet on the other side of the coin their larger cousin, Spanish mackerel, love big baits

THE FIGHT

Spotted mackerel have a fighting style that is relatively easy to predict. They scream off in a straight line for about 30 to 50 meters with incredible pace. Then they go into a dodge and weave routine with heaps of direction chang-

Spotted mackerel landed on a pilchard trolling rig.

es. The cunning ones will run straight back at you, giving the impression the fish has been dropped. Plenty are lost at this stage because if your line loses tension it gives them a chance to spit or shake out the hook. Much of their fighting ability is determined by the line class used to catch them. If for example you use 15kg line with an honest drag setting then an average fish of 4kg will still take line from the spool, but it's very one sided and the fish will soon be bullocked to the side of the boat. Heavy line gets them in quicker, but having a fast swimming fish still full of energy on a short lead does present a difficult gaff shot. Sometimes on the smaller ones we use a net.

I prefer to target them with 6kg line because it lets them strut their stuff and when you have them boat side they are far easier to gaff. They are clean fighters and it's very rare for them to run you over reef. However, anchor ropes are becoming a bigger threat each year as more anglers target them. New chums plus old hands who are plain arrogant, anchor too close to other boats to try and muscle in on the action. I've seen up to 40 boats fishing a small section of reef and when this happens using light line is hopeless. When the crowd gets bad I go off on my own and drift.

When spotted mackerel are on the bite the action is fast, furious and really exciting. It can also be incredibly frustrating when one or two boats are obviously cleaning up while no-one else is getting a touch. This happens regularly as they can hold in a very localized area. Try to resist moving in too close to other boats as you will only cop abuse and that's not what fishing is about.

Just when you think you have them figured out their preferences will change. Some days strip baits will catch heaps and live baits are ignored. Other times without a live slimy you are not in the race.

BURLEY

Spotted mackerel respond extremely well to burley and when they come in, they are not boat shy at all. We have regularly had them cruising around only meters from the boat. They seem to do this more when the ocean colour is

Note the lead on this rig to get the bait down deep.

a deep blue, or maybe it's just easier to see them in that colour water. Burley seems to keep them near the boat for a lot longer when you are drifting rather than anchored.

The best way to burley these fish is with a burley bucket at the back of the boat loaded with fish frames, old bait or pilchards etc. It's ok to add chook pellets to bulk up your burley because the pellets help bring in the baitfish, but mackerel do prefer a fish based burley.

When you are working the burley through the pot, don't flog into it like a mad man because the excess noise can put the fish off. It's better to stir the mix and occasionally munch it up with a minimum of noise. To keep a constant burley trail, this needs to be done on a regular basis.

I use an onion bag on a short rope half loaded with old pilchards from previous trips. Squashed up and dropped over the side they create a constant trickle of pilchard bits and I'm positive they attract spotties and keep them in the area. This bag is set so it dunks itself in and out of the water as the boat slops from side to side. If it was set further from the boat it would get in the way when trying to land a mackerel.

TABLE QUALITIES

To my way of thinking mackerel are an excellent table fish. Some people think their taste is a bit strong but I like them. To keep them in prime condition they should be quickly bled by cutting their throat then stored in ice slurry in a long esky or fish box. For short periods of time they can be stored in a wet hessian bag, but you'll need to be home very early to keep them at their best.

It's easy to see why these fish are so fast.

They have an excellent recovery rate, i.e. the percentage of boneless fillet compared to original body weight. When preparing the fish I fillet off a whole slab from each side then cut these fillets in half long ways by removing the small bones and red meat from where the backbone was. The rib bones are also filleted out. Finally the skin is filleted off by placing the slabs skin down on a hard flat surface, then running the knife between the skin and the flesh. It takes a bit of practice but it is easy when you know how and a sharp knife is essential.

Some people take the easy way out and slice them up into cutlets, although this leaves the skin on and every cutlet has bone in it. If your family is like my mob then fish with bone in it is treated as if it was poisoned. I don't mind eating around bones so after filleting I break up the backbone into 3 or 4 frypan size pieces. Cooked on a BBQ or fried in a pan, they taste great and there is a surprising amount of flesh on it. I realise this will sound really strange to a lot of people, but give it a go, you'll be amazed.

Mackerel is an excellent fish to freeze as it does not lose any of its qualities and it doesn't thor out soggy like some other species. With no bones you have plenty of cooking options. We use it in fish burgers, mornay, deep fried or simply slapped on the BBQ. I am not a fan of baked mackerel. I think it tastes best thinly sliced and fried in olive oil. Remember that if you eat a Spanish mackerel that weighs over 10kg, you are taking a chance on ciguatera poisoning.

These spotted mackerel hammered full pilchards.

CONCLUSION

I've chased mackerel for the last 30 years, mostly from someone else's boat. I've never missed a season, yet every year I still get hyped up and keen as mustard as mates and I follow reports of them coming down the coast.

Mackerel have so much going for them. They are big fish that are great on the plate and you don't have to travel far to find them. Their clean fighting style allows you to target them on reasonably light gear. The challenge and excitement of finding, hooking and landing them is very real, yet they are a lot easier for success than jewfish or LBG fishing. Mackerel also have the blinding speed to get your reel's ratchet screaming like very few fish in the ocean, and they are one of my favourite fish.

NORTHERN BLUEFIN TUNA

Northern bluefin tuna, often called long-tail tuna can occasionally be found roughly a 100k's south of Sydney, up past Brisbane and right around the top end. They grow to 1.5 metres and reach around 35kg in weight. March is the best month for Sydney and the further north you go, the more prevalent they become. In Morton Bay the season starts late September and goes for months as these are a warm water fish.

The fight of a northern bluefin can best be described as huge. They are really fast, often with a long opening run followed by more good runs and a never-give-up attitude. The stamina of these fish is unbelievable. When you work them close to the boat they are still a long way from being landed as they go into a circling routine around the boat. A few are lost at this stage due to line fatigue, yet more gain their freedom by anglers losing their patience and increasing the drag pressure.

If you hook one heavier than the line being used, you are in for a memorable fight. Stay calm, leave the drag alone and keep the rod bent with constant pressure and your chances of landing it are excellent. After a hard fight your first sight of these things can be a bit of a deflation to your ego. It's hard to comprehend how something that battled so strongly could be so small. It doesn't really matter if they are 5kg or 20kg; they punch well above their weight.

Oddly enough a lot of boat anglers don't like bluefin. Complaints range from 'they fight too hard' or 'they're only good for bait' (which is wrong) are com-

These fish are all about speed and endurance.

mon. Bottom bashers and mackerel fisherman are the main complainers as many consider the time used fighting them could be better spent catching 'proper' fish. Not me, if I'm fighting a fish that's spinning the reel I'm having a great time!

Bluefin tend to stay within the first few kilometres from the shore, sometimes running as close as the white water along the rocks. This makes them one of the main targets for land based game fisherman and they are also a great option for kayakers hoping to tangle with a big fighting fish.

BAITS

Yellowtail, slimy mackerel, pike and garfish are the most common baitfish used live. Big ones will take just legal tailor and smallish bonito as well. Pilchards are a great bait to fall back on if live bait is too hard to find.

Because bluefin tend to run in the same water temps as mackerel, most anglers north of Port Macquarie rig their baits on single strand wire because they are expecting mackerel. There are a few bluefin specialists who use mono line claiming tuna are 'wire shy', but most run wire and still get a few.

It's always nice to put a big fish in the boat.

LINE CLASS

These fish are clean fighters and if you are really keen you can use light line on them but I don't recommend it. We have caught a few on 6kg line while targeting spotted mackerel. Luckily they weren't too big because as it was they circled the boat 10 or 15 times before we could land them. As you may imagine, fishing at anchor with light line is a nightmare. If bait fishing with light line the ideal reel is a small lever drag overhead. With a lever drag you can pre-set the drag for exactly the amount of pressure, one third of the breaking strain of the line class used. The other bonus with the overhead is that you can wind in without gaining line and it doesn't cause line twist. If you wind in with an egg beater and not gain line then it causes line twist and the way these fish fight near the boat, it's really easy to wind too much while trying to keep pressure on them.

His first bluefin put up a huge fight on 6kg line.

Spending two hours on a fish is not too uncommon and I have heard of a few times where fishermen have chased them with the boat for kilometres only to lose them at the end. If you are chasing them with the boat, remember to keep solid pressure on them, otherwise you are basically playing follow the leader without actually wearing them out.

Hitting them with heavier line shortens the fight which also gives sharks less time to get in on the act. We have gaffed more than one bluefin with a shark fair up its tail and with a short handled gaff, your hand and arm is getting a bit close to the action as well. If your tuna suddenly breaks out of its circling the boat routine and gives you an early gaff shot, chances are it is using the boat as protection from a shark.

LURES

Surface poppers, stick baits, metal slugs, soft plastics and trolled lures all catch bluefin. A lot of anglers target schools of tuna by motoring up-wind of a school then cutting the motor and casting at the tuna. With the wind at your back the casts travel further and tuna often feed into the wind. When it all comes together it seems too easy. Yet other times this style can be hugely frustrating. They don't always take your offerings and quite often they don't stay in the same place for long. The further north you go, the better this style works.

This fish come to the boat early with a shark fair up its tail.

CONCLUSION

Bluefin have a reputation as being only good for bait which is totally wrong. Normally people making this claim have never tried eating one.

To prepare them both sides are filleted off and the ribs plus the small bones that run along the backbone are filleted out. A really sharp knife is needed because the skin is very tough to cut. Once it is boneless, lay the slabs skin down on a hard surface and fillet off the skin. The flesh of these fish is red and good eating, but the really dark stuff needs to be filleted off.

I like it sliced ½ inch thick coated with flour or a seasoning mix and fried in olive oil. For fish burgers this is put on a toasted bread roll with onion, a fried egg and lettuce or rocket and it's really hard to beat. If you're adventurous try 'buttering' the bread roll with honey or vegemite because while it sounds strange, it tastes great.

Bluefin can be poached, used in stir-fry, soups and curries, or battered and deep fried. Tuna Mornay or tuna parmajana is also an excellent option.

A Moreton Bay tuna caught spinning with a little metal lure.

OFFSHORE OPTIONS

Reef fishing for snapper is the main pursuit for the majority of offshore anglers, yet you never really know what will be caught and the occasional smorgasbord of other species are a welcome addition.

Apart from reef fishing, there are a number of different options available ranging from luring white water around ocean rocks and islands, to going out targeting marlin, sailfish, mackerel, tuna, kingies or cobia. Concentrating on these larger species takes a bit more effort and certainly more time, but it all pays off when you land one.

Ideally, using a protected harbour or bay is the best way of motoring out to the ocean as it is the safest, and if you have access to one of these sites that's great. Yet on many parts of the coast you basically have one of two options, a beach launch or a bar crossing.

You need a rest after landing one of these.

Whether you decide to beach launch or cross a bar, here are a few hints to make it more enjoyable and possibly save you and your family an unwanted tragedy. Take the time to talk to local anglers and find out the best, safest way of getting outside. There may be shallow reef or rocks to avoid, or you may have to follow an ill defined channel. You won't know unless you ask.

Watch what the locals are doing. If they are holding back, waiting for someone else to take the chance and see how they go, be careful. If the locals are packing up and going home, then it's a pretty good reason for you to do the same. If someone who knows the peculiarities of the area doesn't like it, then someone who doesn't know it shouldn't try it.

To the untrained eye, waves have a habit of looking pretty small and insignificant when viewed from a distance, and it doesn't have to be too far either. Yet I can guarantee those same waves will look surprisingly big when you get amongst them. Once when launching from the beach we had a visitor on board, a local board rider of many years. He was having a laugh at our concerns on the size of the waves. He was seeing sets of waves that were far from big but still able to be surfed. We were seeing some dirty sets coming through; waves you wouldn't want to get caught in.

If it wasn't for a conveniently wide, deep gutter to launch into where we could wait in safety, we wouldn't have made the attempt. As it turned out we did have to wait for a lull (flat period) because there was a pretty ugly set of waves rolling in from out wide. Those same sized waves he was laughing at previously were now big enough to put a genuine look of fear on the board rider's face. When there was a good lull we quickly motored out without a problem, with one very panicky visitor on board. The thing is, he was looking at the ocean and judging it with a surf board in mind, not a boat. It doesn't take much of a wave to give a boat a hard time.

These blokes found a good patch of pearl perch.

BEACH LAUNCHING

Most towns with access to a beach have designated sites for beach launching, generally in semi-protected waters on the beach's southern end near a headland.

Launching an offshore boat from the beach is not that hard, if you know what you are doing. Firstly, a 4WD or tractor is a necessity on sand and even they are not immune to becoming bogged. Try to stay on the hard, smooth sand found closer to the water. Dry, powdery sand is easy to get stuck in and should be avoided when possible.

Soft plastics in natural colours account for a lot of reef fish.

At most beach launching sites it is necessary to drive over a reasonably soft patch to get down to the hard stuff. So before attempting it, make sure you are in 4WD and if necessary, the front wheel hubs are locked in.

Select a low gear capable of towing you and the boat the whole way through the soft sand. It's no fun having to stop half way to find a gear able to do the job. Keep the rev's up and the power on until you are on a more solid base. Dragging a boat and trailer through soft sand drains an amazing amount of power out of the tow vehicle. This doesn't mean to attack it in a mad wheel spinning frenzy, but don't go at it half hearted either.

When you are ready to reverse back and drop the boat in the water, have a quick check that the bungs are in their holes and the boat is not still connected to the trailer by a safety chain, winch cable or a tie down strap. Wait for the water to recede then reverse back far enough to drop the boat into the water, but not too far or the back of the tow vehicle will get soaked and you could get stuck. The idea is to drop the boat in a position where it can be spun around to face any waves and they need a bit of water to do so. When you think you are back far enough, jump on the brakes to slide the boat off the trailer. This is easy to do if the rollers on the trailer work, if not it's a real pain.

If everything goes right the driver will motor off to park the vehicle and trailer while the deckie spins the boat around so the bow faces any oncoming waves. To save getting totally soaked, the deckie should hold the boat in this position by standing in the shallower water at a back corner of the boat, guiding it with sideways and forward pressure to keep the front pointing out to sea. This has to be done until the driver returns, starts the motor and has it warm enough to proceed with safety.

The deckie often gets wet and when there is a dirty little shore dump, it's not unusual to get wet up to your chest. This is not a lot of fun at daybreak in winter, but a spare change of clothes or putting up with the discomfort is a small price to pay to get offshore. When the 'boat holder' gets the hang of it, they probably have a 50-50 chance of getting their shorts wet so it's really not that bad.

Deciding whether it is safe enough to venture off the beach is a task often taken too lightly. Some days it's obviously safe with a flat ocean right up to the sand, yet mostly it's not so obvious. Surfboard riders are a bad sign. If they can ride the waves then you can bet they will have some power in them. If you have to punch through these waves to get outside then give it a miss and try some other form of fishing.

As a rough guide, if the waves are one metre or more in size then it is too big to attempt. One metre may sound quite small, especially if you have a good sea boat. But you have to remember that most times you are running in shallow, aerated water where your propeller can't get a good grip so your available power is extremely limited. When a wave is building in front of you and it's ready to break, the water your boat is floating in gets shallower as the wave sucks it out from under you.

Venus tusk fish, sometimes called 'parrots' are great on the plate.

In extreme cases the boat will bottom out on the sand, leaving you at the mercy of the waves. This happened to a mate and I at Hat Head one competition day. We were half way across the shallow creek bar when the water sucked away leaving the boat virtually high and dry. Three little dumpers quickly rolled through and each one of them sent water over the windscreen and into the boat. We were soaked and had a fair bit of water on board, but after the waves there was enough depth to float and we motored out to safer water to bail out the boat. We were the first to launch that day and after seeing our dilemma, a number of competitors gave it a miss. These waves were less than one metre in height and at no time did I feel in danger, but it was still a rough old way of getting out.

When you have enough depth to get power on the propeller it's a good idea to pop it up on the plane and get out past the last line of waves. Quite often

Two huge Pearlies put a smile on this bloke's dial.

you will have to go over a green back wave (one that hasn't broken) and the best line of attack is to approach them virtually straight on. Keep the power on until the boat's bow is riding up the wave, and then back off a bit on the throttle. The reason you have to 'back off' is because if you don't, the boat will launch itself out of the back of the wave like you wouldn't believe.

Most roll-overs on the beach occur when anglers push their luck a bit far. The general plan is to warm the motor, the deckie climbs in while pushing the boat into deeper water, then wait for a lull in the waves. Preference should be given to motoring out through a gutter where the wave action is smaller and the water deeper. These gutters are often formed by a rip.

The calm period during the lull has to be judged by looking out to sea in search of any sets of waves that could present a problem. A lot depends on

Jigging for kingfish needs quality gear and a strong back.

how far you have to travel to get out of the danger zone. Cold motors, engine or steering breakdowns halfway out, or over enthusiastic anglers oblivious to the danger are the main reasons for boats getting tipped over.

Often it's not the first wave that does the damage. It's the second or third big one lurking behind the first wave that cleans them up. If you do get caught out and have to face a wave that is almost breaking, it's best to hit them with enough power to hopefully push through the top half of it before it breaks. If the wave was tall you can expect to land with a thump, hopefully pointing in the right direction with all crew members still hanging on tight. Be prepared to hammer down hard enough on the throttle to maintain the boat's forward motion as you may still have to face another few waves. All this drama can be avoided if you don't 'take the chance' in the first place.

Every wave is different, yet they all react according to the bottom structure they are running over. Some hold up quite steeply for a heart stopping amount of time, while others quickly build up and dump. Developing the ability to 'read' waves is not that hard if you take the time to study them. Boardriders and experienced rock fisherman often have uncanny skills when it comes to reading dangerous waves or knowing exactly where the last part of the wave will break. It's because of the practice and time they put into it.

Catching big fish out of kayaks takes skill.

(Photo by C. Garrick)

Boats to 6 metres, both glass and tin can be launched off a beach. Cats are the most difficult on a beach because they take a lot of water depth to float. Obviously heavy 6 metre craft will give more problems and they need more water to float in but the trade off is a more stable, seaworthy craft once you get out there. For years we beach launched a heavy 5.6 metre glass boat that carried 100 litres of fuel, an auxiliary

141

motor plus a 150 hp motor and did so on a regular basis.

Low tide gave us problems because of a lack of water depth and often we had to wait for more water while lighter tinnies were getting out with ease. A big high tide also gives trouble as it tends to push the tow vehicle up into soft sand. Apart from the state of the tide, we've had troubles with the trailer sinking in the sand while winching on the boat. To get around the problem we used two weldmesh grids which are lined up on the sand so the trailer wheels sit on them while retrieving the boat. If your trailer tyres do bog down, it's better to reverse back enough to pop the tyres out of the hole and then going forward, rather than trying to pull them out while going up hill.

One big advantage with beach launching is the fact that most of the professional fleet use river bars to get offshore. By going off the beach you should be able to fish reefs that don't receive as much pressure as those closer to more popular exit points. Beach launching also gives a fairly good indication of offshore sea conditions. If the beach is rough then chances are it will be sloppy and uncomfortable outside.

BAR CROSSING

Many of our river-bars are quite dangerous and even the 'tame' ones claim lives. More often than not, these lives could be saved if common sense prevailed. The next bloke who sprouts off about how he towed his boat 600 kilometres to go fishing and a bit of bad weather won't stop him, only to be rolled and battered on the bar, will sadly not be the last. River bars deserve respect and a conservative attitude, if there is any doubt about the bar being up a bit, give it a miss and don't go out.

Long toms jump all over the place and are sometimes found in good mackerel water.

One of the most common mistakes made with bar crossings is people not knowing the state of the tide and how to use it. A rising tide helps smooth the bar and gives it more depth. This doesn't mean you can always get out on a rising tide because obviously there could still be waves. But if it looks too big on a rising tide, the bar will be real ugly on the run-out tide.

The run-out tide, especially the last half of the low tide, is the most dangerous time to attempt a bar crossing. Water pours out of the river and boils through the bar, causing sharp pressure waves to form. For some boats these pressure waves are dangerous enough to swamp them, and when mixed with any swell coming in from outside it can become a lethal combination for even larger more seaworthy craft.

The run out tide is causing this trawler some troubles.

Most times it's best to come back in on the same line you went out on because with tides taken into account, you should have a fair idea of the water depth. If there is a swell rolling in and it's forming waves, get at the back of one and follow it all the way across the bar. In turbulent water you often have to juggle the throttle to keep the right position on the wave. The idea is to stay at the back of the wave without screwing on too much power and going over the top, especially when the wave is about to break because they do have a tendency to pull you up onto them at that stage.

REEF FISHING

Fishing the bottom, or bottom bashing, is a time honoured style that is almost guaranteed to produce a feed. Finding good reef is generally not a problem and both drifting and fishing at anchor are productive. Fish can be

143

found on the first reef, right out to as deep as you care to drop a bait. Some days the bite is red hot but the majority of the time you have to work at it for success.

Jigging can be hard work, but worth it when it works.

Drifting is the best way of landing a wider variety of fish because a lot of different terrain is covered. It's also a good way of checking out new grounds. Ideally a drift should be set over reef or scattered reef as that is where the majority of fish are found. The exception to this rule is flathead as they are often found on sand. A lot of areas have traditional flathead grounds that still produce reasonably well despite heavy pressure.

Fishing while on the drift requires a fair amount of lead to keep the baits down deep. A line that is running almost straight up and down will generally catch more fish than one that is at a wide angle with baits at an unknown depth. This heavier rig tends to put fish off the bite in shallow water but once you get out deep it doesn't seem to worry them.

When a good show of fish are seen on the sounder it is often best to put down the anchor. However, before doing so it's a good idea to estimate what angle the boat will lay. This is generally done by motoring into the wind and or current, dropping the pick and allowing the boat to hang back off the anchor. Done properly the boat should be either over the fish or up current of them so baits can drift down to them. No-one gets it right all the time and it is a lot easier to do if a GPS is used.

At anchor, the amount of lead needed to get a bait down is much less when compared to that used while on the drift. The exception to this 'rule' is in very deep water where no-one anchors anyway, or in strong currents. Generally the amount of lead used is just enough to get the bait down to the bottom, and for you to know it has got there. If a bait has reached the bottom without your knowledge and you continue to let out line, a big bow or belly will form in the line, which is a great way of missing bites.

Everyone wants to catch a big snapper.

By using the lightest lead you can fish within your given situation, you improve the fight of any fish you hook because they are not dragging the extra weight. The delivery system and bait presentation is also better when a minimum sized lead is used to get to the bottom. Sometimes you'll find the bait will reach the deck but not stay there because the current pushing against the line is lifting the rig off the bottom. The choice here is to either move up to a heavier lead or free spool the reel so the bait hits the bottom again.

Baits that lift off the bottom with the current are then free spooled back down again to create a hopping effect and as long as you know when they are hitting the bottom, they can be bounced back a fair way and cover a lot of extra ground. This drop back method is not easy to perfect but it can be a real producer of quality fish. With a good assortment of lead on hand the battle is half won, the rest comes with experience and having a good 'feel' for your gear.

A chunky grassy sweetlip.

DEEP WATER

Deep water fishing is an acquired taste. Once you get use to it and get the feel of what you are doing its good fun, but until then many anglers feel lost in deep water. Back in the old days when nylon line was the only choice, line stretch made bites almost impossible to feel. Braided fishing line has made deep water fishing a lot easier. It has no stretch which means you can still feel what is happening down deep, and because the line is thinner, it takes less weight to get there.

Generally you can feel the lead hit the bottom as line stops pouring off the spool as fast. Yet it doesn't always stay there because it gets pushed up by the current or the drift of the boat. The only way to tell if it is lifting off the bottom is to free spool the rig back down a few minutes after you initially drop down. If it only takes up to about 10 metres of line that is okay but if it takes about 20 metres or more you may have to run a bigger lead. If you have no idea if you are getting to the bottom then you definitely need more weight. Once you get the feel of it, hopping baits back can be a very productive style because you cover a lot of ground, but it all revolves around knowing when you have hit the bottom.

Kingfish go hard all the way to the boat.

DOLPHIN FISH

Mahi-Mahi, commonly known as dolphin fish or 'dollies,' are an excellent sportfish and a viable option for much of the year. When water temperatures are above 20 Celsius then the chances of finding them are good. Dolphin fish love to congregate around floating debris such as logs, wood, fish attraction devices etc. The floats and rope of fish traps are an ideal place to target them and you will know within the first one or two casts whether these beautifully coloured pelagics are there. If they are not at home, it's simply a case of motoring over to the next trap which will be conveniently marked with a flag.

Dolphin fish are possibly the easiest species for offshore anglers keen to try fly-fishing. They are aggressive and very competitive when in big numbers, and you often see them under and around the boat. They are a fast growing, schooling pelagic found in 40 metre plus water depth. They sometimes come in closer, but out past 40 metres is a good spot to start looking for traps and debris. Often the wider you go, the better the fishing becomes.

While dolphin fish can be taken on lures, flies, pilchards and strip baits, they quickly learn that something isn't right and go off the bite. Once they do it's time to either change tactics or move to a fresh location. Their biggest downfall is fresh live bait such as yellowtail or slimy mackerel, which they find irresistible. So much so that if you had a big enough store of quality live baits you could pull them in all day. Yet once a livie has been hit by another fish or it's in a crook condition, dolphin fish are not keen on them.

The average sized dolphin fish caught off the traps ranges between 1 and 3

A nicely coloured dolphin fish.

kilo yet they grow much heavier and up to two metres in length. The larger fish are generally a bi-catch of anglers trolling for marlin or yellowfin tuna. Once hooked they turn on the action with good little runs and plenty of head shaking jumps. This ballistic attitude doesn't stop once they are in the boat and if they have any size about them, they can be a real handful.

Some people consider dolphin fish to be excellent eating but I don't think they are very good at all. This makes them a good proposition for catch, tag and release. The fact they have not been pulled up from the depths means their survival rate is excellent as long as they are not deeply hooked because when they bleed, they bleed a lot.

TUNA

Many anglers tuned into bottom bashing pass up a golden opportunity when schools of tuna are working the surface. I've seen boats actually change course to go around a huge flock of birds diving into water boiling with thousands of feeding tuna, yet they never stopped and had a go at them. It's almost

A nice long mahi mahi, commonly called dolphin fish or dolly.

like they have tunnel vision as they motor out to a favourite reef.

The most common tuna found are bonito, striped tuna and Mac tuna. Bonito and Mac tuna are often encountered within a few kilometres of the shore while stripped tuna are generally out wider. Bluefin and yellowfin are the biggest tuna available.

Mack tuna fight really hard for their size.

The quickest way to scatter, and put tuna off the bite is to roar straight into the school. A much better way is to approach them from up-wind, then cut the motor early and drift down onto them with the wind while casting lures at them. Tuna often feed into the wind and with a bit of luck they will come toward you. When the school is big (a few hectares) and there is plenty of baitfish for them, the school doesn't seem to move around much at all and you can drift with them for what seems like ages. Yet the more common scenario is smaller schools boiling the water in short bursts as they herd bait

149

schools to the top then massacre them.

Metal slugs, pilchard imitations and fair sized bean sinkers painted white are all excellent lure choices, as are stick baits and fairly heavy weighted plastics.

A beautiful big tuna.

They cast well and tuna like them. A quality eggbeater reel matched to a two metre casting rod is the best way of delivering a lure out wide. Overheads designed for casting will also do the job and once hooked up I much prefer the overheads fighting ability. Yet on most boats your casting swing is restricted in some way with rods, aerials, the cabin and people getting in the way. It's much easier to flick a lure out with an 'odd' cast using an eggbeater and get away with it than doing so with an overhead. Excited anglers, restricted casts and overheads often result in a fuzzed reel.

If the school is big then you can virtually cast anywhere to score a hook-up. When the school is smaller you'll need to aim the cast to get results. Ideally the lure will land out past them so it can be run back through them. Each school reacts differently and if they are travelling fast you'll need to cast in front of them as well, so they reach the lure while you retrieve. The general style used while casting lures to tuna is to wait a few seconds after it has hit the water to let the lure sink, then wind in with a fast retrieve with the rod tip held low as this helps to keep the lure in the water. Generally a lure running in the water will catch more fish than one skipping over the surface. Yet if deeper run lures are not attracting strikes then by all means run a few over the top and see how you go.

The strike can come the moment the lure splashes down, half way or in close to the boat. Most strikes occur a fair distance from the boat and when the hooks sink in you'll know you have a hook-up. Often you're spinning the reel handle really fast and all of a sudden it just stops dead. You feel good weight and the battles on with plenty of line ripping off the reel. On a weight ratio basis, tuna are one of the most exciting fish in the sea with plenty of spirited runs and a never say die attitude.

Because tuna schools often don't stick around for long, it's handy to have a rod pre-rigged with a casting lure. That way you can be in the action straight away instead of wasting time digging around in a tackle box. Having one or two ultra fresh tuna on board will definitely improve your chances while bait fishing for reef fish, and catching the tuna is a really enjoyable diversion, plus they are also good for catch and release.

Amberjack are an extremely hard fighting fish.

CONCLUSION

It's best to have an idea of what you are going to chase and rig your gear to suit, before you get on the water. It's ok to have a plan B and C because the weather and sea conditions can change, but punching out into the ocean with no idea on what you will fish for is a recipe for failure.

Sometimes we plan to break up a trolling session by doing an hour or two of bottom bashing so we bring a rod each especially for it and it's amazing how invigorating the change can be. Stumbling on working schools of tuna can ramp up the excitement on a reef fishing trip.

Keep it safe and have plenty of food and water. Spare sunscreen and hats, plus extra wet weather gear stored on board can extend your fishing time and keep the experience enjoyable. Remember also that it doesn't have to be a marathon to be a good fishing trip.

Cobia are renowned for putting up a hard fight.

A quality king fish caught on a jig.

A nice sweetlip from a little boat.

Caught off Nambucca and great on the plate, this Gold Spot Pigfish took a bait intended for Snapper.

SNAPPER

The snapper fishery between Brisbane and Sydney is a good one and I believe it to be fairly healthy. Brisbane and the Moreton Bay area produce more big reds than Sydney's offshore.

Of all the offshore species available, snapper would have to rate as the most popular. They put up a good fight, look great and are excellent on the table. Snapper are said to live up to 35 years and fish of 1.3 metres weighing 16 kilo have been recorded. An average fish ranges between half a kilo and three kilo.

There are many localized nicknames for different sized snapper such as old man, reds, pinkies, cockney bream, squire and even snappery squire. I call them all snapper, although with big ones, 'red' may sneak in occasionally.

Snapper have a habitat that ranges from close to the shore to out wide in 200 metres water depth. They prefer reef areas, gravel patches, drop offs and pinnacles plus sandy areas around broken reef. Snapper are often found around the edges of reef and on the down side of the current. While they are generally considered as bottom dwellers, they sometimes have a habit of cruising mid water. These fish are often a quality size and being well off the bottom generally means they are in a feeding mode.

This 7kg snapper fell to a halved pilchard.

They can be caught all year from a wide range of locations although they do follow a loose pattern of heading out wider during the winter months. Cold water tends to slow down their bite and outings where a lot of morwong are landed (a good sign of cold water) are regularly quiet days for snapper.

BAITS

Snapper are opportunistic feeders that will take a wide range of baits. Fresh strips of fish flesh are ideal, especially if they have high oil content. Mullet and tuna are an excellent choice because of their oil although species such as sergeant baker should not always be over looked.

I love the colours of a good snapper.

Small squid or octopus put on the hook whole can be deadly bait and have accounted for a number of decent sized fish. Strips of larger squid are effective as well. Snapper also take pilchards, live baits, prawns and even pink nippers.

Cuttlefish is excellent bait for deep water because it is a nice bright white and is easily visible. It has the advantage of being tough so pickers can not quickly rip it off. The last thing you need while fishing deep is to lose a bait as soon as it reaches the bottom, which can happen fairly regularly with pilchards. A good mix in deep water is a strip bait of flesh on one hook and cuttlefish strip on the other.

My all time favourite snapper bait is mullet because it is a rare day when they turn their nose away from it and I've caught some brilliant fish with it. My largest snapper to date is 9.5 kilo and it fell to a mullet strip. Pilchards come in a close second and strange as it may sound after praising mullet, whole pilchards tend to attract the larger snapper.

With strip baits many anglers make the mistake of trying to thread the bait onto the hook. This results in a bruised blob of flesh that is not terribly appetising to the fish and often the hook point becomes buried or fouled in the bait and can not actually hook the fish. The correct presentation of strip bait is to pass the hook once through one end of the bait, starting on the flesh side. This leaves plenty of hook point showing and gives good presentation of the bait. It has an excellent hook-up rate and does not spin when lowered or retrieved.

This fish took a live, slow trolled slimy mackerel.

THE BITE

Snapper bites range between a subtle bump to a huge thumping run, depending on how they are feeling and the size of the fish. Big fish hammer the bait without warning and are easy to hook, yet some days the more common pan sized variety can test your skill to the point of frustration. I've had inexperienced anglers argue the point when they were told they had a bite because they failed to feel or see that a fish has had a go at their bait. If they weren't told, I'm sure they would have sat there for the next half an hour waiting for a bite without bait on their hook.

Big reds like this go amazingly hard on light gear.

Reels are fished in gear and the drag plus the flex of the rod is often enough to set the hook. Even so I still lean back on the rod to make sure the hook is set. If a rod is in a rod holder and the tip bumps, it's best to pick up the rod, wind in any slack and feel the line as you hold the rod tip low. If you feel more weight than normal strike up with the rod and watch the rod tip for any live action. If it's a good fish you'll soon know and even small ones give indications of their presence.

ON THE DROP

Occasionally you'll find a cooperative school of fish where there is enough competition for them to rise well up in the water column to be first to your bait. Catching snapper on the drop (while the bait is descending) is incredibly exciting fishing. You don't hook every strike because the reel is in free spool, but they hit it hard and when the spool bounces into life it gets the blood pumping.

Under these conditions overhead reels are superior. As the bait descends you have to lightly thumb the spool to stop over-runs, which gives an excellent feel of what is going on. It's also easier to time the strike to the exact point when you want to hit them, which is something that can not be done with eggbeaters. Originally I clicked the reel in gear and then lent back on the rod but found I wasn't hitting them at the exact time I wanted. Now I dump an educated thumb on the spool and strike with the rod, and then put it in gear. If it's a good fish it will scream off taking line with it. That's where the educated thumb comes in with enough pressure to hook the fish yet not enough to break the line.

Big snapper often form quite a lump on their head.

Burleying with cubed pilchards is an ideal way of assisting a school to rise to your baits. Once the bite hots up and there is two or three anglers fishing the rate of burley can be slowed. This is because of the burleying effect created by the baits being busted up as they are hit by fish. It should be noted that the burley rate is slowed, not stopped.

BY-CATCH

Most offshore bottom bashers go out with the idea of catching snapper but in reality you never really know what will take the next bait. Sometimes snapper are the only species caught while others a huge variety of fish can be landed.

The tactics and baits used for snapper are effective on most offshore species, especially those attracted to reef. Problems generally only arise when a really big fish takes a bait intended for something much smaller and the angler's gear is not up to scratch. Many times it's not the breaking strain of the line that fails but rather a lack of length held by the reel.

An excellent eating sized fish.

Sometimes you get blown away on the bottom with a short explosive run without a glimmer of hope of stopping them. Samson fish, kings or amber-jack are often the culprit and it's not necessarily huge fish doing the damage. These fish fight incredibly hard and when they are in a mean mood they fight dirty, quickly running for reef. Snapper are pretty good at this tactic as well, especially on shallow reefs.

The next snapper fisherman to hook a marlin will be far from the first or last to do so. Often the fight is short and one sided. Snapper rigs were never in-tended to stand up against the abrasive bill of a marlin. Yet occasionally lady luck smiles and the marlin is landed. A mate of mine hooked and landed a broad bill swordfish in 18 metres water depth using a strip bait intended for snapper. These fish are more common out past the continental slope and many game fishermen consider their capture as a pinnacle in their sport. This only enforces the notion that you never know what, if anything, will take the next bait.

FIGHTING STYLE

Snapper have a fighting style that sends very characteristic bumps up the line and experienced anglers can confidently predict what is hooked well before it's seen. Unless they are big, snapper aren't a problem to land. They bump around down deep and give a reasonable account of themselves but an average sized fish is no match for the line classes generally used on them. The best way of getting them into the boat is with a large landing net.

Releasing a quality red.

Big snapper are a different story as they can and do run hard and fast down amongst the reef. Yet not all of them do this which is a strange twist amongst the species. There seems to be two distinct groups of big snapper. The first are the ones who try their hardest to bust you off on reef and heavy line is needed to stop them. Even with 15 kilo line there are no guarantees as they often only have to run a few metres to find something to bust you off on.

The second group are very forgiving and elect to fight in clean water. Quite often they can be hooked close to the reef yet they swim away from their safe haven and regularly rise well up from the bottom. These fish are not being pulled away from the bottom, they swim away from it.

These two different fighting styles make it very difficult to select a line class when targeting big snapper. On light gear they perform brilliantly when fought in clean water, but it's incredibly frustrating when they smash you off on the bottom within moments of the hook-up. On the other side of the coin big snapper hooked on stump puller gear are virtually winched to the top and while they still look beautiful, it can be a let down to be involved in such a one sided fight. This is especially relevant if you have previously been successful on big snapper.

RIGS

There are a number of rigs that work on snapper and the right choice between them depends on water depth, current strength and whether you are drifting or anchored.

The little reel's line load was lowered considerably by this fish.

The most basic is a small ball or bean sinker running directly to a hook. This rig is improved immensely by employing a doubled main line of a metre in length with the aid of a spider hitch. The doubled line gives insurance against the line rubbing against teeth, gill plates and the fish's head and body. Sometimes a double also helps when they run down amongst the reef. To get the most benefit from a double, tie the hook on, don't loop it on. A

162

knot means both strands of the double are holding the hook. These rigs are often used as 'floaters' and have the added benefits of being reasonably snag proof. The running sinker rig works well in shallow water and when there is little current out wide. It's an easy rig to make and is my favourite on snapper.

When the current is running and a large sinker is necessary, letting the lead run directly to the hook is not a good idea as it baulks the fish and kills any action the bait may have. A better option is to use a swivel as a sinker stopper and to also help prevent line twist. Ideally the line between the swivel and hook should be heavier than the main line and about half to one metre in

Just how I like them, big and ugly.

length. This is a good rig when the fish are touchy although it does tend to snag the bottom if you allow it. To get around this problem drop the bait down until the lead hits bottom then wind up a bit so the bait can hang down without touching the deck. This rig is most often used at anchor, yet it still works on the drift as long as the lead is heavy enough to easily reach the bottom.

The two hook dropper rig sometimes called a paternoster rig works best in deep water or while drifting. Usually a large snapper lead or bomb is set on the bottom and two droppers or loops are tied at half metre intervals up from the lead. Originally this was the standard rig used offshore and it had plenty of success but nowadays they are not too effective until you get out wider.

The size of the hook used is dictated by the bait. 1/0 and 2/0's are ideal for strip baits of mullet because these baits are relatively thin. As long as the hooks are strong it doesn't matter that they are small. Strip baits of tuna often need a 4/0 because tuna baits are generally thicker, although they can be trimmed to size. Pilchards are best on one or two 6/0's so there is plenty of hook point showing. What-ever hook is decided on it must be sharp and placed in the bait so there is plenty of hook point available to grab the fish. Hooks that are buried in the bait have a low success rate and there is nothing to gain by hiding them.

A quality Moreton Bay snapper.

RODS

Newcomers to snapper fishing nearly always choose a rod that has a far too heavy action. Rod manufacturers continue to mark rods 'snapper' when to be honest; a lot should be marked 'stump pullers'. I like a rod that produces a good bend when I'm hooked up because it helps hold tension on the hook. On a lot of rods with a line class marked on them, I go for a slightly lighter rod than the line I intend to use. For example a few of my rods that I run 8kg line are marked as 6kg rods and I regularly run 6kg line over rods rated as 4kg.

BURLEY

The use of burley will definitely increase your catch, as long as it is used in the correct way for the circumstances. Burley buckets on the back of the boat are virtually useless when the water gets much depth about it or there is a strong current running. The particles forced through the holes are often small and fluffy, causing them to drift away quickly in the current. Burley buckets work best on the close reefs, especially when used in conjunction with heavier burley such as chopped pilchards.

9.5kg snapper caught on a strip of mullet and 6kg line.

There are a few ways to get burley down where you want it in deep water, with a number of burley bombs on the market capable of doing the job. However, I believe the best way is to make your own by mixing smashed fish frames, old bait, pilchards, chook pellets, tuna oil and wet sand. This mixture of whatever is available is placed into food containers and frozen. Chinese takeaway containers are an ideal size and shape for home made burley bombs and as long as there is enough sand in the mix and no air bubbles, they have an excellent sink rate. Obviously you pop the burley out of the container before dropping it over the side.

Half a dozen frozen burley bombs stored in the esky gives you the option of bringing fish towards your baits when fishing at anchor and can make the difference between an average and a great day.

GOING LIGHT ON SNAPPER

Snapper on light gear is an exciting form of sportfishing available to most offshore fisherman. I've had a lot of luck with this style and it's the one I like most. One to two kilo fish become more of a challenge and peel line on a regular basis. When a big fish is hooked the stress levels become pretty high and you'll probably find yourself wishing you were connected with heavier gear. Yet for many, the greatest thrill in fishing is in the battle and uncertainty over the outcome.

There is a real sense of achievement felt after landing a snapper equal or heavier than the line class used. Doing so is not really that hard if patience and constant pressure is applied. Mates and I have found the hardest and most time consuming part of catching big snapper is getting them to bite in the first place, then finding fish that are not too mean. Meanwhile we have a ball and heaps of practice on fish that would otherwise be skull-dragged to the top on heavy gear.

There are no hard and fast rules on what constitutes light line. For some anglers the idea of going under 8 kilo is ridiculous yet some of the good snapper specialists in our area use 3 kilo line and manage reds over the old 10 pound mark (4.5kg) on a reasonably regular basis.

6 kilo is a good line class for an introduction to light line offshore. There is a surprising amount of stopping power in 6kg, yet there will be times when line literally pours from the spool. If 6 kilo line sounds too light then try 8 kilo for a while and see how it feels.

For a typical offshore snapper trip I take two 6kg and an 8 kilo outfit and these do most of the work. Occasionally I also take my 15 kilo whopper stopper gear but it doesn't get used often. If the fishing is slow then I'll work all the rods, but once things get a bit hectic only one or two are used. The reason I cut back on rods is because sometimes it is physical impossible to keep bait up to three rods and in the panic to try and do so, you miss good strikes and actually catch less fish. When the fish are biting it is far more productive to concentrate on one or possibly two rods.

The boats I fish from are well equipped with rod holders so we can work a number of rods each with safety. On the odd occasion I'm on board a craft with limited or no holders then I cut back rod numbers accordingly. There's no future in fishing with a rod that is only leaning against the gunwale. Sooner or later it will be lost which is a bummer, and it's not fair on the fish. Over the years I've seen a number of unattended rods rocket over the side because of a good strike. A good rule of thumb is when there are no spare holders, don't put out extra lines.

LIVE BAITING SNAPPER

While mostly caught on pilchards and strip baits, snapper are also a predator and will freely take live bait. Small to medium sized yellowtail, commonly called yakkas are prime live bait for offshore work. They are an extremely hardy species that can handle sudden depth changes without a problem. On the extreme end of the scale, we've dragged yellowtail down deep over reef in 80 metres of water and on retrieval they were still very lively.

When fishing with live bait the expectation of a big fish is high, so I send them down on the heaviest gear I have at the time. Even though a live yakka

A personal best for this young bloke.

tends to weed out the bigger fish in the school, the majority of snapper we get on yellowtail range between one and two kilo. As with any bait you can only catch the fish available. Apart from the possibility of a big snapper, the reason for the heavy gear is that you could catch anything ranging between a sergeant baker to a marlin. Although kingfish, cobia, amberjack, jew, samson fish, pearl perch and teraglin are more likely.

Deep water live baiting is done with the use of heavy lead. The rig is either with a big 'snapper' lead on the bottom with a dropper roughly one metre up from the lead, or a large ball sinker, swivel, then almost half a metre of leader to the hook. Ideally the leader (line from hook to swivel) could be a bit longer but if the bait has too much room to swim, lines begin to tangle.

On the close reefs live baits can be successfully fished deep under a float. If for example the reef is 15 metres deep, then set the float 10 or 12 metres from the bait. Knowing how to tie a float stopper knot is really handy at this stage, otherwise a cube of styrofoam is connected to the main line. To do this, run a knife slice all the way around the foam then half hitch the main line twice around the cube, making sure the line goes into the knife slice. If the line doesn't go into the knife slice there is a good chance the line will break when you get a strike.

When fishing live baits under a float, I prefer to do so without lead and let them find their own depth. If you especially want to send them deep then a bit of lead can be used but keep it light, otherwise the action of the bait will be stifled. If for some reason a heavy lead is needed then a swivel one metre from the hook makes a good stopper for the lead. This allows you to use a heavier leader line to the hook and also gives the bait a bit of room to swim.

Remember that if the lead is too large there is a chance it will 'pop' the float, and when you do get a hook-up that lead will be heading for the bottom. This is especially relevant when the bait has been sent out in the current for a fair distance and a styrofoam cube or balloon was used. When these floats pop free from the line there is a reasonable amount of slack line in the system. This keeps weight off the hook and allows the fish free line to run to the reef.

A torpedo float threaded down the main line and a chunky float stopper knot is a better option than a styrofoam cube. Apart from the obvious littering aspect, a torpedo float provides a bit of resistance, keeping the line reasonably tight and pointing towards the surface. Using the knot of a long leader line is another way of 'stopping' a float.

The size of the live bait doesn't seem to worry snapper, especially if the reds are big. I've caught snapper down to 1.5 kilo on pike that were over 30 cm long. These baits were intended for Spanish mackerel and fished on wire and gang hooks. Interestingly, all of the smaller snapper I've caught on pike had hit these large baits just down from the back of the head, taking the last hook of the gang. This is possibly the first killing blow when the bait is too large for the fish attacking it. However snapper over 5 kilo have no such problems.

Floating live baits out over shallow reef is an excellent way of covering a lot of ground away from where the boat is anchored. It can also be practiced on the drift.

TARGETING BIG SNAPPER

For reasonable success on big snapper you definitely have to target them. The vast majority of reds over the old 10 pound mark are landed from the close reefs within 3 kilometres of the shore. The odd one comes in from out wide, but not too many.

The close reefs are the place to be and while it's nice to have a big reef system to hunt over with the sounder, small isolated reefs are also productive.

Don't be deterred if the reef is only a few hundred metres from the beach because these places rarely see a fishing line and are often visited by larger predators including snapper.

Early morning, late afternoon and early into the night are prime times to chase big snapper. Boat traffic often puts them down so a quiet, out of the way place is preferable but not essential. Summer and autumn months are the most productive yet looking back over the years in my diary shows big snapper caught from the close reefs during every month of the year. So if you put in the time, sooner or later you'll get one. Heavy weather or strong southerly winds tend to bring them in close as does local flooding.

Many anglers try, but few land snapper of this calibre.

Many anglers consider the close reefs to be full of rock cod and other rubbish and in some respects they are. If your baits are sitting on the reef or are just above it you can be sure of catching heaps of rock cod. A better way is to have the bait right up off the bottom, or slowly drifting down on 'floater' style rigs. Floaters are lightly weighted baits (or no weight) designed to slowly and seductively waft down through the water column. They may or may not reach the waiting rock cod, but their slow descent gives quality fish more time to find the bait.

Working the sounder takes a lot of the guesswork out of whether there are large fish on the reef. When one or two big fish are seen and you get the anchor down, a good strike can come quickly. It's handy to be prepared because often the first good bait over the side is the one that gets hammered. This has happened to us on a number of occasions and should not be ignored. You don't get too many shots at good reds and anything that increases your chances is worth a try.

I prefer to use the sounder aggressively and if we have fished a feature such

as a pinnacle for half an hour without a strike, I reckon it's time for a short move to another part of the reef. Other anglers prefer to find a feature, usually from past experiences, and even if it's not showing fish, anchor for hours and try to bring them in with burley. These blokes do have success so it's not a bad idea if you have the patience and are confident with the spot.

A Queensland summer snapper.

Big snapper are like a magnet for anglers and if you let it slip over the radio that you have caught one you'll soon find yourself surrounded by other boats. Under these conditions it's rare another will be landed. Although you can be sure that a few of those boats have marked your secret snapper spot on the GPS and it will be fished hard at a later date. When you do get a big snapper it's best to be a bit vague about where it was landed.

CONCLUSION

If you are lucky enough to hit a school of large hungry fish, try to keep the blood lust to a minimum. It's fine to take one, possibly two trophy fish but more than that is being greedy. Snapper are slow growing and the large ones are super breeders producing huge numbers of eggs. They are also survivors of better times. Because of their breeding potential I wouldn't be surprised if in the future a maximum size limit was placed on them.

The old idea that you have to 'bag out' for the day to be a success is changing. Hopefully this is because angler perceptions are swinging towards a more conservative attitude rather than a lack of fish.

TARGETING BIG FISH

The water between Sydney and Brisbane holds some really big fish that are rarely easy to catch. It takes a whole lot of things to come together for success and with one weak link in the chain; it can all come tumbling down.

The term big fish has different meanings between anglers. The Holy Grail for bass anglers is 50cm, and then they let it go. Years ago, jew (mulloway) fisherman chased a 50 pounder, but now many dream of a 30kg monster. Some anglers simply want a feed and anything bigger than legal is welcome.

A reel's ratchet screaming into overdrive is a sure sign of a big fish, especially with a correct drag setting. With line pouring off the spool there is very little you can do except hold on, enjoy the experience and try to control the adrenalin rush.

The temptation to crank up the drag is huge but you've learnt from hard experience that's a disaster waiting to happen. Suddenly there is nothing. No weight, no roaring reel. You wind flat out in the hope the fish is swimming towards you but there's nothing. You've done another one.

Every time this happens something dies deep within. Your confidence is torn to shreds by self-accusations and it seems the bigger the fish, the bigger the crime. Fishing mates and onlookers mumble their condolences, taking great care to avoid eye contact. There is nothing else to do but finish winding in and check if the hook pulled, the line broke or worst of all sins, the knot came undone. Does this sound familiar because it used to happen to me.

Many anglers bring bad luck on themselves by fishing with inferior gear. Reels that are badly maintained generally have a lumpy drag (one that does not release line smoothly) and are sometimes even hard to wind. Most people who use this sort of

This monster sized mackerel is what dreams are made of. (Photo by L. Williams)

gear only realize it is faulty when they start fishing because they never think to check the equipment before going out. The chances are also pretty good that a badly maintained reel is only carrying half of its line capacity, and the line is probably so old that the owner doesn't know what breaking strain they are fishing with. Any one of these things can tip the scales strongly in the fish's favor, even before you wet a line.

Good maintenance and planning go hand in hand. If you were hoping to catch your very first marlin and you owned the gear to do it; wouldn't it be a natural reaction to check the condition of the reel, the drag, the line load and the rod guides? You bet, and you would have probably spent the last few days tying and re-tying leaders, sharpening hooks and the 101 other things that need attention. All of this sounds pretty normal for marlin, yet the same principle applies to any style of fishing. Even if you simply hand line bream from the shore, the small amount of gear needed still has to work to be effective. You still have to plan ahead and put as much as possible in your favour to have regular success.

Big Samson fish put up a hard fight.

When that long awaited massive hook-up does occur, don't blow the chance by doing something dumb. If the fish wants to run then let it. The reel's drag is designed to release line under tension and as long as there is a reasonable length on the reel, a running fish is still under control. Some people, especially those who haven't experienced many big hook-ups, fall for the trap of thinking the drag must be too loose and that is the reason they are losing line. So they either tighten the drag or thumb the spool, both of which generally end badly.

Half of the problem is caused by a momentary disbelief of any fish that big being foolish enough to take your bait. Rash decisions are easily made during the adrenalin pumping pressure of an unexpected run. If you can stay reasonably calm and don't do anything radical then the chance of a capture is pretty good.

Keep the rod bent at all times to keep constant pressure on the hook. This applies for the duration of the fight because a lot of fish are able to spit, or shake a hook free when they get a bit of loose line to work with. Short stroking or the pump and wind methods of working the rod have their place, but the most important thing to remember is to always have the rod bent and gain line when-ever you can.

Just about everyone involved in fishing would have heard stories of whiting or bream fisherman who hooked and eventually landed a big jew. While the actual hook-up may have been a fluke, the capture was definitely not.

Big fish can make you smile for a week.

These anglers would have had their scary moments where they were tested to the limit, but they stuck to the golden rule of being conservative and staying connected. Even though they were obviously under gunned they concentrated on the task of angling, and were rewarded with a good fish.

Far too many people when confronted by a big hook-up dismiss it as 'just another ray' and pop the line so they can get back to serious fishing. You may have your suspicions as to what is on the other end, but you never really know until you see it. A mate of mine hooked what he thought was a stingray and he very nearly popped the line. He was lucky that he never because the 'stingray' turned out to be an 18.5 kilo jew, the biggest fish he has ever landed.

Apart from the angler, the weakest link in any fishing system is the knot. For this reason, particular attention should be paid to their construction so they are tied correctly. There is no need to learn a heap of fancy knots to be a good fisherman, but you do have to know good knots. By saying good knots I mean ones that never ever slip.

Over the years many fishing writers have extolled the virtues of the blood knot or the 'locked' blood knot and some even show diagrams of how to tie them. Consequently the blood knot is a popular connection. I reckon these blokes have a lot to answer for their actions. To be totally fair it must be noted that some of these writers make mention of the fact that the blood knot is prone to slip. Which begs for the question of why teach a fisherman a knot that slips?

Even the word 'locked' in the locked blood knot is a contradiction in terms and very confusing. The locked blood knot is still prone to slipping, so it's not really locked at all. Generally, yet not always, it slips under periods of constant pressure, just when you need it the most. Another insidious thing about these knots is when they slip, they don't always leave the tell tale wiggly end of a failed knot.

A nice wahoo that fell to a trolled skirted lure.

Undoubtedly some anglers reading this will think I've been too hard on blood knots, but consider this. I've been a fishing nut all my life. I grew up on a diet of fishing magazines and books with pages full of massive fish. I wanted to catch these big fish so badly I could taste the action. So when diagrams of the locked blood knot were published a number of times, I figured this had to be the right knot.

Caught in 20 metre water depth, this yellowfin tuna was 'shortened up' by a hammerhead.

They worked fine on small fish such as bream and flathead, but on the odd occasion I did score a big hit something always went wrong. I'd sink in the hook, have a great run of about 30 metres and then drop it! This went on for years because big hook-ups were few and far between so my base of knowledge was limited.

It was easy to make excuses such as the fish reefed me or there must have been a weak spot in the line. When confronted with a pigtail end on the line, I felt like a real dope who couldn't even tie a proper knot. Sometimes I just couldn't find an answer because I was sure I'd done everything right. It couldn't be the blood knot because all of these fishing writers obviously knew more than me. I still shudder when thinking of the fish I had dropped by using a crook knot.

Just to muddy the water a bit, I have two mates who use locked blood knots that don't slip and I have no idea why! Yet I know numerous people who use the blood knot and it does slip, but most of them won't admit it. Sometimes there's an amazing amount of 'bite offs' in a day, all on the other bloke's line.

For me the turning point came when one of the top anglers in our fishing club showed me how to tie a uni knot. He explained to me that the locked blood knot was a useless connection because they sometimes slip. To be honest, at the time I didn't really think his argument was valid. But I was desperate and willing to try anything because I had just dropped a Spanish mackerel and was feeling pretty low. Even so, I still very nearly didn't try the 'new' knot because of blind pride. It's so easy to side step the truth saying 'that's not the problem, it must be something else'.

There is nothing prettier than seeing your first marlin
beside the boat.

Over the next few weeks I gave the Uni knot a good testing and to my surprise and delight, I started to actually land big fish. I was tickled pink! Being brutally honest with yourself can really improve your fishing.

This is why I consider the locked blood knot to be a dog of a thing. It slips. It's as simple as that. And it held me back for years. If there is even a shadow of a doubt about the knots you are currently using then check out the uni knot, snood knot and the spider hitch. They are the best knots that I know of for staying connected.

If after reading this bad review of the locked blood knot and you still intend to use it, try this test. Tie your knot to a hook and leave a fair length of tag end. (The short end) Hold the hook with a pair of pliers and put slow constant pressure on the main line. Gently increase the pressure to the stage where you 'break' the line, all the while watching the tag end for slippage into the knot. Sometimes they let go really quickly and it's hard to see, while others it is obvious.

If you can tie 10 separate knots and they ALL pass this test, then you haven't got a problem and you're probably better off sticking to what you know. But if a few of them slip then give that style of knot a big miss and learn something better.

Once a hard running fish has taken approximately half of the line load from the reel it is time to back the drag off a little, (i.e. lighten the drag) otherwise there is a very real chance of the line breaking. This is because with a lower line load it takes more pressure to pull line off the spool due to having less leverage. Water pressure also comes into the equation.

Knowing how much and when to lighten the drag with hard running fish is an acquired skill. Simply knowing it has to be done is a big start. If you go overboard and really back off some fish will slow down. Others, such as big Spanish mackerel will keep on blazing away, taking your line with them.

There is real skill involved in staying connected to a distant running fish when the line load is really low. All rod movement should be very smooth and if possible standing on a high position such as a headland will keep a lot of line out of the water. Anglers do this to try and prevent water pressure popping the line. This style is used by land based game fisherman targeting big fish, especially when lighter line classes are used.

Big snapper are always welcome on board.

Obviously standing on a headland isn't much help for boat anglers, but they have the option of chasing the fish to regain line. Yet even in a boat I'm not keen on chasing them and only consider it as a last ditch option. It's hard enough hooking something that big and to run it down with the motor seems to me like cheating. Sometimes if you want to stay connected you have no choice, although if possible I rather fight them from a 'dead' boat.

Using reels with a large line capacity, say 500 metres, reduces the amount of times you will have to touch the drag. Very few fish take 200 meters during the fight and with a large line load it still wouldn't be a problem. This isn't to say that bream fisherman should have reels holding 500 metres of line as that would be impractical. Yet it still pays to be over gunned, line-load wise in case something bigger turns up.

You'd have to be happy with this sized wahoo.

Whenever I fish offshore or there is the chance of a big fish turning up, I use either a leader or a double. A leader is a heavier line roughly twice the breaking strain of the main line, connected to the main line via a swivel or two Uni knots. A double is formed using the main line doubled over and tied with a spider hitch. Both a leader and a double are used to combat wearing of the line near the hook from the fish's teeth, gill plates, head and sometimes their tail as well. Sharp teeth such as those of a shark or Spanish mackerel will instantly slice through fishing line so they require a wire trace, which in itself is a type of leader.

Try not to fall into the trap of scoring big fish on light line until you have caught a few with a sensible or even heavy strength line. Once you know how your target reacts and you're comfortable with how they fight, then if you want, drop down and go lighter.

CONCLUSION

When you find out quality fish are on the bite and 'going off' you need to make a real effort to get out there and have a go at them. Life is hectic and there are always heaps of reasons why you mightn't go. Yet if you study the really good anglers in your area, you'll find they make the effort to get out and put in the hours during prime time when the fish are there.

Facebook has made information gathering so much easier than it was in the old days. There are plenty of brag boards and speciality sites with a lot of people willing to help. Don't ask for specific locations, especially for bass because that sort of information is usually guarded.

Once you get on the grapevine it's a two-way street so add to the gossip yourself but again don't brag about all the bass you caught in a certain creek, because that will put you offside with every angler that fishes that water. Common sense is needed because if you were fishing with 50 other boats then it's fine to mention the location.

No-one is born a magnificent angler and in this sport you never stop learning. Persistence, attention to detail and learning from your mistakes is what makes a good angler. Studying other successful anglers' styles and questioning them as to why they do certain things will also put you on track. Even when you are blown away by something big, and it will happen, if you learn from the experience you'll have a better chance of landing the next one.

THE MIGHTY MULLOWAY

Mulloway, commonly known as jew, jewies or jewfish, have a wide ranging habitat from out wide in the ocean, up rivers almost to the brackish water and everywhere in between. They can be found in reasonable numbers from Sydney to Brisbane and can be caught 365 days of the year.

The nickname 'jew' is said to come from the otalith or jewel, taken from the head of a mulloway that a lot of anglers use to keep as a trophy. I've always known these fish as jew or jewies and I will probably always keep calling them that.

According to the book Australian Fisheries Resources, mulloway grow 2 metres in length and the heaviest recorded one caught in Australia weighed in at 43 kilos. Yet the same species to 71 kilo have been landed in South Africa. These things grow big and that's a huge part of their appeal. They also grow quite fast with some on the NSW North Coast recording

2cm growth per month.

Apart from land-based gamefishing, these are the most challenging fish you will ever target, especially if you are starting from scratch. The best way to fast track your success is be incredibly lucky. Otherwise put in the time at locations with a good track record with quality heavy gear and preferably fish with anglers who have cracked the 'jewie code' for that location.

One nickname that has come into vogue during the last few years is 'silver

ghost'. This has a lot of merit because when you first see them it's a huge flash of silver coming out of the depths. The ghost part is relevant because you can put in a lot of time without seeing one. If you are the type of angler who has to catch fish every time you go out, then jew fishing is not for you.

Most successful jew fishermen specialise in a specific style and area. I know less than a handful of anglers capable of consistently catching them from offshore, the ocean rocks, off the sand, river breakwalls and boating in the river.

That's a nice fish from a kayak. (Photo by C. Garrick)

Ideally you should target one or two of these options that are best suited for you and give it a solid shot for 12 months. Keeping and entering a diary every time you chase them is an excellent way of finding patterns on what locations fish best at what tide, moon, weather conditions and bait used. Note time of hook-up, bait, state of the tide and anything else that is relevant. Some of my entries note location, tide, moon, bait and NBJ when I catch

Breakwalls in winter are often productive, but cold.

nothing at all. Some excellent computer software based fishing logs have been released in recent years.

THE MOON

Given a choice I prefer the time between a new moon up until a day or so before the full moon. Yet I know some excellent jew specialists who believe the dark period before the new moon is by far the best. Other blokes, whose opinions I respect, swear that a few days after the full moon is the best. It's all very confusing because different locations fish better at different times and tides.

One thing's for sure, if you haven't got a line in the water, you won't catch one.

BAIT

These fish are fussy feeders and many anglers believe live baiting is the only way to target them. While there is a lot of truth in their belief it is not quite correct as plenty have fallen to dead baits.

Top quality bait is essential and fresh is better than frozen. Fresh octopus and squid are excellent dead baits and are mainly used whole, although if they are too big then large strips or single skinned tentacles are ideal. Octopus is an extremely tough bait that resists hordes of pickers for a fair amount of time, which is handy when the 'rubbish' fish are thick.

A quality 'city' fish. (Photo by S. Santoro)

Fresh slab or strip baits of mullet, tuna or luderick (blackfish) are excellent baits. If there are very few pickers I like to use big baits because I think they are better for big fish. Yet when pickers are fairly thick I'll use one of the pickers for bait, or cut back to reasonable sized strip baits and change to a fresh one fairly regularly. It is frustrating when your baits are being torn up but the smell and commotion caused by this action can bring in the bigger fish.

Dead bait-fish can be rigged whole, filleted or 'butterflied'. To butterfly bait, the tail and most of the backbone is cut out. This results in a solid bait with the head and chest section, plus two wings of flesh that move about and release burley in the form of oil and juice. The main thing to be careful with butter-flied bait is to make sure the wings cannot foul or cover the hook point.

When tailor are a kilo or more I consider them too big and hard to handle as live bait. Some anglers may disagree with that statement because a big jew has a huge mouth that is easily capable of swallowing a kilo-plus tailor, yet it doesn't suit my style of fishing. With the big ones I generally take two slabs off the sides and use the head and shoulder section as well. This gives three quality baits and is a system regularly used by many of the top jew fisherman on the north coast. This style of getting three baits works with freshly caught luderick as well and jewies love them.

A quality fish on a bright sunny day. (Photo by C. Garrick)

Shop bought bait such as mullet, tuna, squid and octopus can be used as either the main bait or as a backup in case you can't catch something fresher on site. Even if it is backup bait, it still pays to buy quality fit for human consumption. This can be obtained at fishermans' co-op's, fish shops and some bait shops. To keep it in pristine condition, storing it on ice in a small esky is ideal.

Baits used for jew are much larger than most anglers are accustomed to and it pays to think about how you want the bait to be presented before madly sticking hooks in it. Ideal bait presentation is where the bait is well secured, neat, not bruised, with plenty of hook point showing in such a way that the bait cannot fold around the point. Burying the hook in a large bait is the most common mistake made by anglers using slab or butter-flied baits. Sure the hook has to hold the bait but there must be plenty of hook showing for it to be able to hook the fish. Careful bait preparation is one of the stepping stones towards landing a big one. These fish do tend to turn you into a perfectionist.

PROSPECTING WITH PILCHARDS

Many breakwall and rock fishermen don't realise just how effective a well presented pilchard is for jewfish. On a number of occasions where I've successfully landed one, nearby anglers have commented how it was such a 'lucky' capture on a pilchard.

This fish was caught off the ocean rocks on a pilchard fished without lead.

Luck be blowed! I target jews with pilchards and they work. If I'm lucky enough to catch a tailor then it quickly goes back out on the heavy gear as either a live bait or large strip bait, but as soon as the first pilchard hits the water, I'm fishing for jews.

I've called it prospecting because that is exactly what you do. Search the water and fish holding structures with an unweighted pilchard, working the area hard until you find fish. Toss the pillie all over the place, find the direction of current flow and make it work for you by drifting the bait over reefs and holes. Places where white water spreads foam over a deep hole or gutter are ideal. Without lead bait can be cast into, and slowly worked over incredibly rough territory without the worry of instantly snagging the bottom.

If snags do become a problem there is a way to further reduce the chances of hooking reef. It is by burying the gang hooks straight down through the back of the pilchard. This way the only hook point showing is the one that goes through the eye sockets. (The one closest to the fishing line) While I generally prefer to have plenty of hook point showing, this system of hiding the last few hooks still works. Pilchards are very soft bait and when a jew hits them, they bust up pretty well which releases the hidden hooks. When using this system it pays to give the fish a little bit more time to take the bait before hitting them.

The feeling of a jew taking a pillie is generally a fumbling sensation, similar to the bumps of a bream but not as sharp. Any strange bream bites should be treated with the suspicion and respect a big fish deserves. Wind up any slack line and if you feel live weight then belt it. If it's a bream you'll probably miss, but if it's a jew be prepared to instantly lose line because their first run is very powerful.

A soft plastic caught jew off the ocean rocks. (Photo by D Clarke)

Occasionally they give no indication of their presence and all of a sudden you are hooked up to a real screamer. It's great when this happens and the chances should be good that the hooks have already found their mark. Yet I still strike at them to be sure I've popped the hooks in. Over the years I've dropped a few of these sudden screamers due to the hook or hooks pulling out. My hooks are always sharpened so the only explanation for this that I can think of was that the hooks didn't actually bury into the fish in the first place. By all means strike at the fish but never, ever lockup on them. A solid sharp lift of the rod will set the hook, even when the fish is taking line.

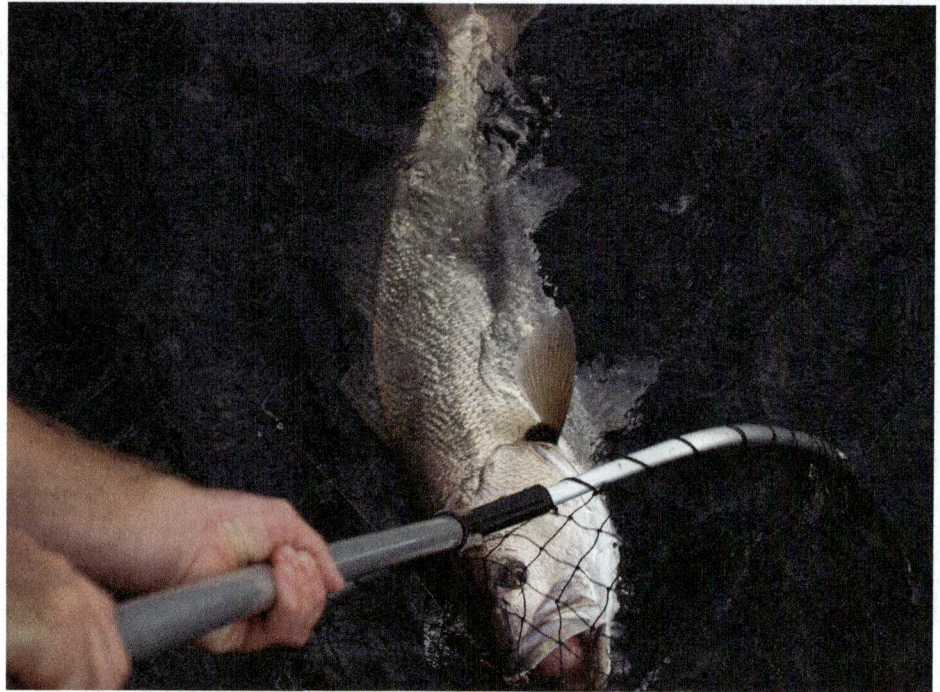

A solid, large landing net makes boating fish a lot easier.

When using a pilchard on three ganged hooks, I prefer to cut the tail off just behind the last hook. Pilchards cast a lot better without the extra wind resistance of the tail and when it's in the water, oil and juices seep out of the cut which produces its own burley trail. This burley trail is only small but it does add to the chances of success. The down side to this practice is that tailor prefer the tail on the pilchard and if they are scattered and in a fussy mood you may not catch one for bait.

If it is at all possible, try fishing pilchards without lead. Bait presentation is natural and far superior without lead, allowing the pilchard to follow underwater drifts and currents, hopefully to the waiting predators. Very little casting distance is sacrificed and with a bit of practice they can be tossed a surprising distance. Naturally enough extra weight is needed when casting into wind or if the seas are up and there is a strong surge working. Otherwise, pilchards work better without lead.

These size fish go hard on bream gear.

Pilchards are a great backup for when livies can't be caught. They have the advantage of being attractive to larger baitfish such as tailor, salmon and pike so if your hook selection allows, there is still a chance of catching a live bait while still jew fishing.

When I'm chasing an each way bet of either a jew or a quality bait such as tailor, I use gang hooks in the pilchard. If bait fish have been non-existent then I prefer a single 9/0 hook because it is far stronger and has a better hook up rate. You can also load it up with 4 or 5 pilchards, all hooked through the eye, which makes a very tempting bait for big fish.

LIVE BAIT

While anglers have a number of firm favourites, jew will take a variety of live baits. Mullet, tailor, slimy mackerel, yellowtail, pike and just-legal luderick are hard to beat and should be targeted when chasing livies. Butterfish, herring, garfish and whiting are my next choice. Often the live bait used is more a case of what you can catch rather than what you prefer. Yet if you can catch a big specimen of whatever 'rubbish' fish that is available, you're in with a reasonable chance. Mates and I have caught a lot of jew up to 15kg on butterfish and they weren't our first choice for bait. I once caught a 12kg jew using a 30cm bream, so you never know what they will take until you put it out there.

Livies are either caught on site or carried in and kept in a kids' blow up swimming pool, a plastic garbage bin, an esky, or in buckets. The bigger the bait the harder it is to keep them in prime condition. Don't crowd the bait bucket and if one dies then take it out or the rest will follow suit. To keep them healthy an aerator and regular changes of water are advisable. This water is to keep the baitfish alive and is not to be polluted by washing your hands in it.

Tailor are a regular visitor to the end of the wall and when they have been holding in the area for a few days the chances of jewfish feeding on them are extremely good. Tailor are excellent bait and can be used alive or as ultra

189

fresh slab baits. Most breakwall tailor are only just legal in size and these fish are a very good size for live baiting.

Caught on a herring, this fish put up a great fight on light gear.

Quite often tailor go off the bite once darkness falls. This is strange behaviour, as they generally like the dark. It's possible they just move on but whatever the reason, it has happened enough times on different walls and off the rocks to make us plan night trips so we are set up at least an hour before darkness. This gives an added bonus of acclimatising us to the place we are going to fish. We can see the holes, wave size, slippery rocks; good gaff sites plus a heap of other things and generally gives you a feel for the place before it is dark.

LAND BASED NIGHT ANGLING

Fishing breakwalls or the ocean rocks after dark can be an unnerving experience and should never be done alone. The friendly atmosphere of white water, seagulls and sunshine disappears with the light and is replaced by a sinister feeling of impending doom. Personally I don't mind breakwalls but I'm not a fan of night rock fishing. The dangers involved are very real and I find it takes too much concentration on staying alive to be enjoyable.

Admittedly, I've had some magical nights soaking a big bait. It can be incredibly peaceful with a low swell and plenty of light from a building moon. The stars are bright and sometimes the shooting stars are unreal. These are the

190

nights that keep me coming back. It's the black, dark nights I'm not keen on. On the east coast of Australia all of the 10 nights before the full moon are

good for rock fishing because there is enough light to see. Obviously the available light depends on the cloud cover because it can still get really dark and no matter what the moon is doing, you still need a torch or head-lamp.

It's amazing how many times mates and I have organised a night trip to coincide with a good building moon yet it has still been incredibly dark. You can pick the moon but when the cloud rolls in, it's dark as hell. Waves loom out of nowhere, crashing into

Headlamps are handy for night fishing.

the rocks with a nerve tingling jar. With sight being restricted to the beam of a headlamp, your other senses work overtime. You hear things that go unnoticed during the day, like the sigh of water sucking back through the barnacles and cunje, building into a wave ready to pound onto the rocks. Some nights you can't see them, but you sure can hear them.

The long nights are worth it when you score a good one.

A solid jew caught from the rocks.

When there is enough light to see my line, I prefer to work a bait with minimal lead so it washes around with the surge and current as I believe it presents the bait better and covers more ground. At night this practice is often unfeasible because it can produce too many snags and it demands you move around the rocks quite a bit in the dark. If the sea is reasonably calm and there isn't much current running then a drifting bait can still be used at night, but it helps to have a sound knowledge of the place you are fishing.

The style often used by jew fishos after dark is to use enough lead to hold their bait in a reasonably restricted area. This allows the angler to prop themselves in a comfortable and safe position without the constant worry of their bait being washed back in. Often it's a case of casting out, winding up any slack line, sticking the butt in the rod bucket around your waist and settling back on a comfortable rock to play the waiting game.

If you are keen to fish the rocks after dark then only do so with an experienced night fisherman. Don't even contemplate going on your own because that is total madness. If you still intend to go alone at night then fish the beach, because it is a lot harder to get into trouble and you are still in with a good chance of a jew.

One of the main reasons I don't do more rock fishing at night is because it is hard to find a partner and unless you are in tight with a group of keen night anglers you will have the same problem. Still, plenty of jew are caught early in the morning and late in the afternoon. While it definitely helps, you don't have to fish at night to be successful.

GAFFING

While jew don't have the stamina of a big tuna or the blinding speed of Spanish mackerel, they are still a classy fighting fish. Their first run is extremely powerful and they generally fight until they are on the edge of death. Unlike sharks, they don't save their energy for emergencies and once they are close enough for the gaff there is generally very little fight left in them. They normally just lay there with hardly a flap, as they surge around with the current flow. Yet they are not always easy to gaff and the task should never be taken lightly.

Spinning off the ocean rocks produced this quality fish. (Photo: Greg Hill)

A lot of things go through the gaff man's mind when he's pressured by a big fish. His own safety should be the main priority, and if he considers it too dangerous then he shouldn't do it. Even a monster isn't worth dying for. In some cases, a relatively inexperienced rock fisherman will consider the gaffing location too dangerous. Yet an old hand, (generally the one on the rod) knows he is safe in that location. The thing to do here is to swap the rod for the gaff and let the experienced bloke gaff the fish. Never let yourself be bullied into what you consider to be a dangerous situation.

If you do swap the gaff for the rod, you owe it to the angler to try really hard to stay connected to that fish. At some stages you may think you are going to drop it, but never give it away as a lost cause. You've lost it when the line breaks or the hook pulls, not before. Fortunately jew are pretty placid when they are beaten and they generally don't try any dirty tricks in close. One exception to this 'rule' is when you are fishing with heavy line which gets them in a lot quicker and they are not always beaten by the time you get them at your feet. Under these conditions they can bung on the rough stuff in close.

The long walk back to the car.

One trait of the jewfish that is handy is the fact that when they are totally beaten and have 'had it', they float. They may go under in a water surge or an eddy, but they come up again pretty quickly. So there is no need to bullock them around at this stage. Always keep tension on the line to hold the hook in, but go with the flow of the water as you direct the fish to the gaff man.

When a jew is washing around close to the rocks there is a danger of the line being caught on a barnacle or cunje. Be aware of the problem and try to avoid it by slightly backing off the drag and keeping the rod tip up. If the line does get hooked around a snag during these closing stages, don't panic and do something radical. Often you can free the line with gentle flicks of the rod tip or by using ocean surges to your advantage.

When the gaff man is presented with a shot he should lower the gaff under the fish with the shaft of the gaff between the fish and the rocks. Then sink the hook in with a smooth yet solid lift of the gaff handle. This way the shaft acts as a guide, and the gaff hook should find a deep purchase point. Another reason for having the gaff shaft between the rocks and the fish is that there is much less chance of the fish rolling off the hook when you attempt to lift and or drag it out.

Try to keep both ends of the gaff away from the fishing line because it is very easy to get tangled, especially with the long handled gaffs that are common for this sport. Come in from behind the line and try to gaff them in the gills or chest area as it will help you drag them out. In reality, any gaff shot that lands the fish is a good one, no matter where it hits.

One problem I've found while gaffing jew is when you punch a neat hole through one of their big scales and it gets stuck on the point of the gaff. You can hit them a few times afterwards with what you think is a good enough strike to sink the gaff in, but it just keeps bouncing off. You need to get the scale off the point and then give it another shot. This happened to me while using a long handled gaff on a dark night with a weak torch. I had a hard enough time trying to see which way the gaff hook was facing, let alone see a scale on it. It wasn't pretty, but we eventually landed the fish.

For land based fishing a long handled gaff is a necessity. They need to be sharp and they need to be strong. If a gaff is not capable of lifting a big weight on a straight lift, then it's not really a jew gaff. For very high locations a flying gaff is essential.

WALKING THE WALL

To get around the problem of fast running currents, many breakwall fishermen cast their bait out and walk along the wall at the same pace that their bait is being washed by the tide. This has the effect of holding the bait out from the wall. Although if the water is deep or there is a belly in the line caused by water pressure, the bait will work its way back into the wall's base so you still have to watch what you are doing.

Years ago anglers favoured their bait set under a float, yet the most popular style today is fishing the bottom with a ball sinker running directly to the hook. The sinker size is determined by the amount of current and the size of the bait. Both styles work and each have their advantages on the day.

Floats are good when the tidal flow is not too strong or when fishing over heavy reef areas. They are also good for working baits right in close to the wall. The biggest trick with float fishing is setting the bait (alive or dead) close enough to the bottom to attract fish, yet not too deep to constantly snag. The depth of the rig is set with a float stopper knot, a short length of line tied around the main line so it will hold against the power of bumping through the rod guides during a cast, yet still slide up or down the line so you can change the depth of the float. Stopper knots are basically a set of figure eights (using different line or wool) tied around the main line. When tying a stopper knot, be careful that the main line stays straight and doesn't join in with the knot. Also don't cut the tag ends of the stopper too close as they tend to come undone and without the tag ends, the knot can't be re-tightened.

There are not many walls where you can drive directly to your fishing spot.

If the bottom is reasonably level then finding the right depth is fairly straightforward. Problems begin when the water depth varies greatly along your section of drift. Under these conditions float baits set for shallow reef areas are high in the water when drifting over holes and gutters. Jew often 'hole up' out of the current and baits run past their nose have a far better chance of being taken.

When using a small live bait under a float, it's best to hook the bait just behind the head, preferably where the fins above their backbone begin. This gives a solid purchase point where the hook doesn't have to be too deeply set (always place the hook above the lateral line) in the bait and it also keeps them pointing into the current. If a bait is hooked near the tail and there is much of a current, the bait will quickly become lethargic and soon drown. I prefer to use a small sized ball sinker running down to the hook when float fishing. The idea of the lead is to help the bait to get down to a reasonable depth where the jew are more likely to be, and sometimes more importantly, to give the bait more protection from diving sea birds. This is mainly relevant with small baits such as herring. Under these conditions the trick to using lead is to not go over-board with too much weight.

While walking the wall, there is a certain fishing etiquette that should be followed. Basically it is common sense, courtesy and consideration to other anglers. If everyone cooperates then a fair number of anglers can walk the wall at the one time. Keep a reasonable distance between anglers and if need be, wait for your turn at the start of the drift and don't cast out in front of anyone. When someone gets a big hook-up then that angler has total right of way. If

This trolley made from a golf buggy is used for carrying live bait to the end of a wall and also helps carry out the catch.

there is the slightest chance of your line tangling theirs or getting in their way then wind in and give them a clear run. After all, when you hook a rampaging jew hell bent on bolting off along the wall, wouldn't you expect a clear run?

Good strong live baits are best for walking the wall. When you bump a snag with dead bait there is a fair chance of it staying snagged. It's possible to lift it over the boulder or whatever it has stopped on and with practice you'll get pretty good at it. Even so, you can still expect to lose a lot of gear. The advantage with a healthy live bait is they will often swim themselves out of the snaggy country, which can save a lot of re-rigging. As the strength of the bait diminishes, the chances of a snag increase.

Walking the wall is taxing on livies because they get bumped around a lot down there and they often need to be retrieved and cast out a number of times during the drift. After the same bait has been cast out a few times it's a good idea to re-position the hook in a more secure location. Repeated casts tend to wear a hole in the bait, often big enough for the hook to fall out when there is not much tension on the line. Light gauge hooks with small barbs are more prone to this problem.

These days most walls have flat cement walkways, which are ideal for this form of fishing. This is basically a daytime proposition because unless there is a bright moon you won't be able to see your line and chances are it will wrap around boulders and snags near the water line. Low light periods during early morning or late in the afternoon are ideal and can be considered as prime time. During the day can also be productive, especially if there is heavy cloud cover. I've seen far too many caught during the day for them to be lucky captures. A fair amount of these were landed in bright sunny conditions so while cloud is handy, it's not absolutely necessary.

This 15kg jew fell to a live butterfish while walking the wall.

END OF THE WALL

The end of a breakwall where it pushes into the sea is often quite a productive place to fish. On many walls this is one of the few spots that can be fished at night without baits constantly sweeping into snags. Anglers generally plan their trip to coincide with a run-out tide, as the current tends to hold baits out from the wall.

Sometimes the end of a wall can also be fished on a rising tide but generally only when an eddy is working on the river side of the wall. This doesn't happen on every wall and should not be taken for granted that it will. Occasionally excess water pushing down a river after heavy rain equalises the effect of a rising tide, resulting in very little tidal flow. This can be an excellent time to fish locations that look 'fishy' but are often un-fishable due to the current. Some walls have an ocean side and if the wall pushes out a fair way this can be a good side to fish. There are still effects from tidal changes, although not as radical as the river-side.

Two lure caught jew from the end of a wall on a wet afternoon.

A common mistake is to cast out too far. There is a definite feeling of satisfaction when you throw a huge cast and the bait lands right out wide. Yet the end result could very well leave your bait sitting on a flat sandy desert where you will probably only catch shovel nosed sharks or rays. Jew are very structure orientated and unless there is a series of gutters or a hole out wide, or you are targeting a patch of white water, you are better off fishing in closer to the wall.

Ideally you should try to get the bait in the area where sand meets the reef section of the wall, preferably on the sandy side so it doesn't snag. Local knowledge, using your eyes plus trial and error are the main ways of finding where the sand meets reef. Every wall is different and the bottom structure changes throughout the year due to the large volume of water movement. The reef stays there, but there are always holes and sandbars being formed or torn apart. The end of a wall generally fishes better when there is deep water or a good gutter or hole. Shallow, sanded up sites are not what I classify as prime.

This was by far the biggest fish this lady had ever caught.

One exception to the 'rule' of fishing close to the wall is when tailor have been working out wide as the jew will probably be out there as well, feeding on tailor. If nothing is happening with baits in close, then by all means send one out wide and see how you go.

Fishing the end of a breakwall is very similar to fishing the ocean rocks. Some days the ocean is flat while others it's wild. If the rock you are standing on is wet then chances are you also will get wet. Wave action changes with different stages of the tide and while your spot may well have been dry when you arrived, there are no guarantees what it will be like in a few hours time. As with most things, using common sense and caution is the best way to go. You don't need all of your gear right up next to where you are fishing. If you set up 'camp' 10 or more metres behind you, the chances of it getting soaked by a wave are a lot lower.

BOATS

I started targeting jew in a small trailerboat when I was old enough to get a car licence. The first one I got was about 4kg and I thought it was a monster!

I scored a few bigger than that afterwards but that first one will never be forgotten. Engine troubles put an end to that boat and I drifted to a lot of years being a deckie and fishing the ocean rocks and breakwalls.

I finally got another boat and figured the jew would be a lot easier. I was wrong, they are still hard. Admittedly I did find a lot more up to 12 or more kilos, but cracking the really big ones still remained elusive. To get the reels really spinning I dropped back in line class and had a ball doing it. Yet when the monster turned up I was under-gunned and it rubbed me off on a channel marker 300m away. With heavier line it would have never got that far. It still hurts thinking about it.

Two nice fish landed from a charter boat.

Jewies are very structure orientated so fishing along a breakwall is an obvious choice. They also like old boat wrecks so if you know where one is then that is a great place to target. They are often found in areas with very strong currents which can be extremely hard to fish. Places like the Rip Bridge and the Hawkesbury River, Rail and Road Bridges are famous for really big fish and the water races under all of them. These are not the only ones either, any bridge in saltwater with a good current flow is a prime spot.

The strong currents move a lot of food and jew have a habit of hanging in back-eddies and low pressure zones around rocks, holes and bridge pylons, feeding on what the current brings to them. They also travel a fair bit when it suits them as well, so if you don't score a strike fairly early in your fishing session, later hook-ups are probably travelling fish.

Most anglers target the hour either side of a tidal change hoping the current won't be too strong. This is a good time to fish but with practice you can extend your chances by learning to fish fast currents. Overall, I've caught more jew in fast water than during the calm change of tide.

Live baits in fast water are rigged to face into the current, otherwise they quickly drown. A two hook snood rig is a good one. The lead hook (closest to you) goes through the nose or top jaw and takes the weight while the other hook is pinned down towards the tail. Because jew eat them whole you can get away with one hook, but I'm still more confident with two. Due to their odd shaped mouth, butterfish and herring are not very good for this style. Another place for a single hook in a live bait is just behind the head. Make sure the hook point is pointing up away from the bait, otherwise it could turn in, stab the bait and foul the hook point. If you rig it like this, drop it out and watch it to make sure it is swimming into the current.

A big fish in a small boat.

Sinker sizes vary to suit the current. If it is running hard then a very large bean or ball sinker is needed to get to the bottom. Yet live baits don't have to be right on the bottom for success. One very productive style is to hop the bait back out in the current. You free spool the rig out until you feel it hit the bottom then put it in gear. Often the current will lift up the bait and lead so a few minutes after dropping down, free spool the rig down again. Keep free spooling back every 10 or so minutes and you will cover a lot of ground. When you have too much line out, slowly wind in, check your bait and start again. The same style can also be used with dead baits.

When the current starts to slow it's important to change your lead to a smaller size, otherwise your lead will stay on the bottom and only your bait will drift back when you feed out line, which is a great way to catch a snag. From the bank the change of tide is easy but in a boat, especially if you have too many lines out, it can be surprisingly difficult. The boat swings around on the anchor with every surge of the tide, tangling lines and snagging those with too much weight.

When using heavy line from a boat it is a good idea to have a plastic hand-caster on board. When you get a snag, especially when it is cleanly hooked, it can be almost impossible to break the line. To break a snagged line, wrap the main line a few times around the hand-caster and keep pulling and wrapping the snagged line around the hand-caster until the line breaks. The hand-caster gives you something solid to pull on and saves your hands and arms from being cut by the fishing line.

Electric motors and soft plastics have changed the way a lot of anglers target jew. Now it is common to see anglers drifting along a wall, or using the electric to position in an area while casting plastics close to structures. Most times these blokes also target the change of tide as it makes the whole system so much easier. The plastics are generally, but not always, quite large. This is mostly done during the day. Flathead are often a bi-catch and from Port Macquarie northwards, mangrove jack and estuary cod also come into the mix.

Remember to keep some tension on the line when getting ready for the gaff shot so the hook stays in place.

Check the size and bag limits for your state because even though it may be the biggest fish you have ever landed, it could still be undersize.

CONCLUSION

Targeting jewfish is often a love, hate relationship. It takes persistence, dedication and often a lot of time before things start going right. These are big powerful fish that have a habit of finding any faults in the gear or the angler using it. For most people the amount of hours put in per bite can become really depressing. You don't get many chances so you tend to become a perfectionist, trying to get everything in your favour. Dropping one can make the outing seem far worse than not even getting a bite.

Plenty of anglers target them hard for a few outings then lose their enthusiasm and fish for something easier for a while, before the jewie bug bites again.

Yet when it all comes together and you see that massive slab of silver coming up from the depths, you tend to forget how tough the road was to get there and the world feels great again.

A night time lure caught fish.

ABOUT THE AUTHOR

Steve Flockton is happily married with two adult children and six grand-kids. Even the youngest know he's a fisherman. Steve loves his fishing with a passion bordering on fanatical. He can target mackerel or marlin one day then chase bass or bream the next and have a ball both days. Some anglers consider him to be lucky or even an expert, both of which he strongly denies. His answer is always 'I'm just keen and work hard at it.'

From the age of 6 or 8 years old he was rockfishing with minimal supervision for weeks at a time during school holidays at Avoca. These days it would be totally unacceptable but back then it was no big deal. His passion for wild, untamed places started here and more than 50 years later he has never been washed in and is still good on the rocks.

Steve has competed in local, state and national fishing competitions with quite respectable results. These days he drifts along and fishes the seasons. Mackerel season, bass or bream season, snapper season and drummer season to name just a few. He has fished from a lot of different boats and has crossed most of the river bars between Sydney and Brisbane plus launched off a lot of the beaches as well. His favourite fishing styles cover boating offshore and in the estuary, land based from breakwalls and the ocean rocks, plus lure tossing from a kayak on quiet water. Favourite fish would include bream, snapper, mackerel, drummer, jew and bass. The vast majority of his fishing has been in the incredible waters between Sydney and Brisbane, hence the name of the book.

CPSIA information can be obtained
at www.ICGtesting.com
Printed in the USA
BVOW07s1455271217
6110BVAU00026B/3/P

9 780648 062769